Recruiting with Social Media

Using Social Networks to Drive College Admissions

RECRUITING WITH SOCIAL MEDIA

Using Social Networks
to Drive College Admissions

Dr. Clinton R. Lanier

Printed in the United States of America.

Lanier, Clinton R.

Includes references and index.

ISBN 9780615624631

1. Social media 2. Internet marketing 3. College recruiting 4. Higher education administration

Contents

i

Preface

In 2008 I had the privilege of redesigning the languishing website of the New Mexico Institute of Mining and Technology. I was an Assistant Professor of Technical Communication at the time, and was teaching courses on web design and media studies so I was invited to bid on the project along with a few outside consulting firms.

I won the bid and set about creating a new presence that would really showcase the school. The task, as it turned out, was monumental. The original website was designed circa 2000 and really had not been updated since.

It was, to put it mildly, astronomically out of date.

In eight months of exhausting work my team and I created a brand new website, a new design, a content management system with distributed authorship, and a wealth of new features and functions that would bring the school's online presence in line with its competition.

The plan at the time was to then hand the website over to the new director of web communication—whomever that might be—and then get back to the business of being a professor.

Things did not really happen like that.

Instead I was asked to stay on and direct the website and web communication efforts at the school. So, In August of 2009 I became the Interim Director of Web Communication for New Mexico Tech.

I had not really concerned myself with the entire web effort up until that point. After all, I was only going to create the website and then hand it off to someone else to use.

But, facing the fact that I was in this new position for awhile, and the truth that everything from then on would reflect back on me, I began a brief, internal audit of our web communication and online marketing strategies.

My audit revealed that the school was very far behind in terms of digital marketing. They spent much of their money on traditional marketing devices—brochures, mailers, even billboards—but nothing (not one dime) on digital marketing outlets. So, I made the decision to change this.

I first rounded up all of our social media platforms—those that were already in use—and then created those platforms that we did not yet have.

Our Facebook page had been started, and was being maintained by, a student. So, I took this over and began marketing our presence there immediately.

I created a Twitter account and unified our YouTube presence.

I also began populating and updating these platforms. Our Facebook page began to swell with students and alumni immediately, and our Twitter account is consistently monitored and updated. Our YouTube channel picked up many new subscribers, and I scoured the campus looking for videos and images to upload and share.

From 2007 to 2009 our school—which is a very small and specialized research-oriented university—saw declining enrollment numbers that alarmed our administration and our Board of Regents (which was part of the impetus for funding the project to redesign our website in the first place).

From 2010-2012, however, our freshmen enrollment numbers have reached record levels.

Interestingly there was really no new factor that anyone put into place, other than our web-based initiatives.

I am confident that aside from the new website we created—with all of its positive features—another primary factor affecting the increase was our social media efforts.

Specifically, our interactions through Facebook and the strategies we carried out via YouTube have both boosted New Mexico Tech's presence to a whole different level.

I have filled this book with advice and information drawn from my education, research, and perhaps most importantly of all, my time directing the social media strategies at New Mexico Tech. I hope you find them useful, and I hope they help connect you and the potential freshmen of your school.

As you finish most (not all) chapters, you will also find Action Items, short lists of suggested ways to use the chapter's lessons immediately. Most center on putting the information to action for your school or office, or ask you to consider how your effort fits with the information provided.

Take advantage of these action items and try to really consider what is being asked. Putting the information to use as soon as you can will help you create a solid and meaningful campaign.

x

1 Making College Admission Social Again...

It is hard to think of a more stressful time in a young person's life than the period of trying to decide what college to attend, and then trying to actually get into that college. It is so stressful in fact, that in 2006 the American Academy of Pediatrics warned that the pressures it causes could be detrimental to the health of teenagers.

It is not so much getting into college, but getting into the "right" college that causes the stress. Pressure from family, friends, and the potential for future employment, put untold amounts of strain on the mind of a high school student.

The college admission process certainly does not help. Universities weed through potential applicants, selecting those with the right test scores, GPA, and academic and extra-curricular activities.

The university admission office plays a strange role in this mechanism. At the same time counselors are both gatekeepers and marketers. While trying to attract more students to the school, they are also charged with admitting the "right" students—those with acceptable test scores, etc.

The life of a college admission counselor can be very demanding. According to one counselor, who blogs about her activities as a for USC, a typical day goes like this:

"wake up before 7am, visit 4 high schools throughout the day, maybe squeeze in a late lunch or nap, head to a college fair, try to eat a healthy dinner, sleep in a hotel, repeat" (1)

She also goes on to mention that she spends a grueling 2-3 weeks on the road on these recruiting trips.

From what I have seen in my experience, this is certainly typical. Making this even worse are the hassles of the "typical day": Setting up and taking down tables at college fairs, shipping or hauling around college viewbooks and materials, the constant grind of selling, and on and on.

And what is the potential student's typical day like in this process? He or she gets to talk to the counselor for a few minutes, given some literature and paperwork, and then on to the next one.

And, chances are, the potential student does not even read most of the literature he or she is given, nor does the conversation with the counselor really affect their decision.

According to a 2010 report by Noel-Levitz, 75% of high school students look at a college's website to determine if they want to go there. Further—and more to the point of this book—76% of high school students use Facebook to help them determine the college they want to go to, and 80% use social media websites (blogs and other sites) to gather information about a college (2).

Meanwhile, schools are spending ever more in their attempts to attract these students (some studies suggest up to $2000.00 per entering freshman).

And while new technology is introduced at a break-neck pace—in the form of smart-phone apps, virtual tours, and online conferences—the old methods of recruiting are still used just as frequently.

There could and should be better ways to recruit, and one of them—the one this book focuses on—is through social media.

As we will see in future chapters, social media is a system of personal communication. It has the potential of placing admission counselors and high school students in close (virtual) proximity to create real relationships, not the brief encounters typical of the recruiting trips most counselors go on.

While many counselors may meet potential students at a college fair or other in-person activity, such activities—by necessity—are very brief and limited in time. Social media has the power to expand the amount of time counselors and potential students (and their families) spend with one another.

Imagine the positive outcomes this can have. Not only will students and counselors build relationships based on trust and the sharing of important information, but it will help them make choices that directly impact their future.

I do not think anyone would argue that it would be ludicrous for any student to make his or her decision based on the combination of a brief meeting with a stranger, and the little information found in a brochure or pamphlet. But that is exactly what happened up until about seven years ago.

Now, as previously mentioned, students have the power to find out about a college through other methods, all based on the internet and the many tools it offers.

Would it not be more valuable if the college admission process embraced this and put every effort into making it the center of a new type of counseling and recruiting?

This book can help you do that, by discussing the important and "need-to-know" information. You will find out where your target audiences are spending most of their time online, who they are talking to, and what they are being told.

You will also learn how to use the new tools and platforms to help students get through the process. And you will in turn learn how to use these same mechanisms to help you recruit more students that fit the profile your school is looking for.

By the end of this book you should have a solid grasp on what social media platforms to use, why you should use them, and how to use them effectively.

There is certainly no guarantee that these mechanisms will help you achieve whatever goals you have set, but at least they will place you in the same environment as the people you are trying to reach.

2 Defining Social Media

Before we start, let me ask you a question. I want you to write down your answer, and then at the end of the chapter I will ask you to look at it again to see if it needs to be revised.

Quiz—what is social media?

- Is it Facebook and Twitter?
- Is it a new way to communicate?
- Is it a new way to advertise your school?
- Is it something only your students use?

Now, turn the paper over so you are not tempted to change your answer and let us get started.

So what is social media? To different people, the term "social media" means different things.

Some say it is what kids and people with too much time on their hands do.

Maybe it is a bunch of different complicated programs on the web where people put up random trivia about their lives.

Or social media is something that always changes and is impossible to keep track of.

In a way all of these are somewhat right. Social media *has* been around for a relatively short while, so its predominant use is by younger demographics.

On the various platforms people *do* seem to use it to inform us of quite trivial things that most probably would not care about (who cares what kind of coffee you like, right? And please do not tell us about your bathroom experiences…).

And yes, platforms *do* seem to come along pretty frequently and then disappear from sight with little more than a whimper. And this does make it difficult sometimes to keep track of what we should pay attention to and what we should not. After all, only five years ago, MySpace was IT, and now it is gone the way of the abacus.

But in truth none of these is *quite* right. Each may capture a portion of the concept, but the definition of what social media 'is,' is actually quite complex.

Social media guru Brian Solis, who has been helping many of the top brands like Nike and Coca Cola use social media effectively, defines 'social media' as a fundamental shift in the way we communicate. He goes on to explain that social media creates a democracy that allows consumers to broadcast and distribute their message as only certain institutions used to do.

In other words, social media has nothing to do with specific tools, or the people that use them, but instead it is the potential for using technology to have our own voice in an arena we used to not be heard in.

Here, I will give you a brief, but personal example of what he means.

About 10 years ago my wife filled up her car at a gas station owned by a particular gas company in Carlsbad, New Mexico. She drove about four or five blocks before the car died and the engine light came on.

We had the car towed to the nearest station that could work on it (it was a Volkswagen and the nearest certified mechanic was 200 miles away).

After looking at the engine, they determined that there was a significant amount of water in the fuel system, and the engine had to be extensively cleaned and the gas tank drained and cleaned.

The whole thing set us back about $500 or $600 dollars which was a lot of money considering we were students at the time.

Now, anyone paying attention can figure out that the gas station was the culprit. So I phoned the station, got the number for the district manager and gave him a call. He took down my details and said he would get back to me.

A couple of days went by when he called me back and stated flatly that it was not their fault—they had checked the gas in the tanks and there was not any water in them. If I wanted to contact them further about it, I would have to go through their legal department.

Case closed.

We had no place to go to voice our side of the argument, and hence, nothing got resolved.

Now flash forward to 2011. It is late one evening and I am trying to stream a movie on Netflix, but it keeps stopping and cutting out on me. I have my computer in front of me so I send out a quick tweet to my thousand or so followers.

> Geeze Qwest, What's the deal? Cannot even watch a movie because my connection speed stinks.

Then I turn off Netflix and go about trying to find something worth watching on cable.

Story over, right? Well, not this time. Within a couple of minutes I am notified that I had been mentioned on Twitter (a mention is when someone else sends a tweet with your twitter-name in it).

Upon investigation, I found that I had been mentioned by the Twitter account for the customer satisfaction team at Qwest—my internet service provider. The tweet said,

> @ClintonRLanier Hello, If you are having speed issue all the time, we can take a look. talktous@qwest.com or follow and DM@talktoqwest

What an amazing change!

Only ten years ago, businesses could get away with treating customers the way we had been treated by the gasoline company. After all, what could we do? What recourse did we have?

Let us think about our options for a moment. We could have written a letter to the editor of the local newspaper, but IF it was published it would have been read by a very small population. What is more, once it was published its life was over—it did not live on past the printing.

As an aside we did write a letter, but the editor chose not to publish it because it was essentially our word—or more likely the word of the technician at the VW dealership—against the gas company. Basically the paper did not want to get sued.

So other than letters and emails to the company itself, and short of legal action, there was really nothing my wife and I could do, and the company knew that. That gave them the freedom to write off our concerns and dismiss our problems.

But in the next example, Qwest recognized the potential I had for broadcasting my unhappiness with their service. In fact I did just that, and in seconds over a thousand people saw my message. If any of them had chosen to send my tweet to their followers (known as retweeting), the number of people that could have possibly seen the message grows exponentially.

So Qwest did what brands and companies must do today, they engaged with me and created interaction.

Lesson 1: Social Media Democratizes Communication

Social media then, aside from the platforms and the way some people choose to use it, is the potential for the common person to create and broadcast messages in the same volume that ten years ago could only be achieved by newspapers, magazines or television (i.e., standard media).

Qwest was only reacting to the potential I had for negatively impacting their business. They did not reach out to me because of some corporate altruism (not to sound too negative), but because they knew my attitude towards them could be broadcast to thousands upon thousands through social media.

I want to take a moment to look at two other cases, because I think they provide truly outstanding examples of the power of social media, and how it has changed communication.

The first took place in 2007. That is when a Georgetown University law student named Brian Finkelstein caught his cable repairman asleep in his house. He took a short video, put some music to it, and then uploaded it to YouTube.

YouTube
sleeping cable guy
Browse
A Comcast Technician Sleeping on my Couch
DoorFrame
Subscribe
2 videos
0:30 / 0:59
Like
+ Add to
Share
1,699,365

Video of sleeping Comcast technician (notice the number of views!). From www.youtube.com

The video had over a quarter of a million hits almost overnight. The story ran on local and national news stations, and Comcast had a PR nightmare on its hands. Within weeks, other videos featuring sleeping Comcast employees made it to YouTube as well.

The original video has now had almost two million hits, and Comcast has had to ramp up its customer service strategy, using Twitter and other social networks.

The second example also involves YouTube, but in this case it was not a sleeping cable repairman, it was a normal guy by the name of Darren Bryant. Darren was fed up with what he called Bank of America's, "phone maze." He needed a decision to be made about one of his accounts, but could not find anyone who could do it.

Frustrated, he uploaded a video to YouTube in 2009.

"The reason I am making this video," he said, "is to get in contact with someone from Bank of America who can make a decision."

In the brief 4 minute video he walks viewers through his problem, then includes his email address and phone number. Finally, he sent an email with a link to the video to about 20 Bank of America email addresses he found on the web.

Within four hours, Bryant received a phone call from a Bank of America executive who helped him solve his problem.

Social media creates power for the consumer and customer, replacing the power of the corporation and standard media.

And to truly understand and use social media for university recruitment, you must start by understanding that it is a new method of communication, one that puts the customers, in this case the students and their parents, in the position of media creators, not just consumers.

They can create information about your school and then share it with the rest of the world.

They can learn about your school from students like themselves—from what those students have created and shared.

They also expect to communicate like this now. They do not read viewbooks, brochures, postcards or flyers. They communicate socially.

Lesson 2: Social Media is Communicating Socially

Think of it as how we communicated 100 years ago.

In the early 1900's there was of course very little of what we would consider mass media. Even the newspapers of the day were very local and featured little in the way of global or even national news.

When the domain for news is that small, EVERYTHING is news, but not just through the newspaper.

Let us say for example that you live in small town America of 1911. You have certain stores you shop at all the time, and Butcher Bob's is one of them.

But then, all of a sudden, Butcher Bob's meat quality goes down. In an instant everyone in town knows about it. Why? Because you tell everyone at church, at the local cafe, at school meetings, and at community events. The people you tell then tell the people they know. And before long, Butcher Bob is rushing to try to sway public opinion back to the positive.

He might reach out to you and let you know that he is only carrying the best quality like he used to. He might make friends with the town's gossip and busy body and spend time showing her how fresh and lean his cuts of steak are (knowing she would then tell everyone within earshot about it).

He might start running specials for the customers he has had the longest to make sure they stick around and in the hopes they will spread the word to their friends about how good Butcher Bob is treating them.

In short, his reputation and his business depend on the word-of-mouth.

And this is how business communication used to be. Businesses built a clientele that was loyal and spread the word about that business. Marketing was minimal and instead time and resources were given to creating a network of dedicated customers who would go only to a certain market and not others.

And what is more, those customers talked to each other. Everyone knew each-other's business because of word-of-mouth.

Then along came mass media and the talking stopped.

But the advent of social media has created the opportunity for us to communicate like we used to do. However, the "community" we talk to is potentially global. And ultimately word-of-mouth communication about people, businesses, products, services and brands, is becoming more important than the traditional forms of marketing and advertising.

While I might see a product advertised on television, I will buy the product because my best friend just did (and then posted it to Facebook telling me that it is the greatest thing since sliced bread).

So that is what social media is: it is a democratizing of communication because it provides not only a way to create a message (all media does that, after all), but it creates a system for anyone to distribute and broadcast that message.

And social media is also a way to communicate socially, just like we used to do a century ago—through word-of-mouth and personal recommendations and referrals.

So pull out your quiz, how did you do?

Next we are going to spend some time on the various platforms that make up the *media* part of social media.

Action Item

1. Think about the students you are trying to recruit. What do they talk about on a social basis? Fashion? Technology?

2. Do some research online to find out what the trending topics were on Facebook and Twitter for audiences in the age range of your students. What did you find?

3. Think about their parents now. What do they talk about on Facebook and elsewhere? Do the same kind of research but for

users in the parents' age range. What do you find for this audience?

4. Write all of these answers down, and be ready to do this kind of research throughout your use of social media.

3 The Platforms we call "Social Media" (the important ones)

Now that we have a better understanding about what social media is it is time to take a look at the various platforms that communication through social media (otherwise known as social communication) takes place on/through/with.

In this chapter we are going to cover a few of the basics: some platforms you are familiar with and some you may not know. We are also going to talk a bit about how they are used and what makes them social. In the next chapter we take a similar look at other social media platforms, but they are not nearly as important as those we cover here—which you will be much more likely to use in your campaigns.

In later chapters we will cover the specifics of which to use and how. Think of this information as just a 10,000 foot view to get the lay of the land so to speak.

And even though those we cover in this chapter are more useful than those in the next, it is also important to remember that not every one of these will or should be used by you and your school in its recruitment efforts. Each platform has its own strengths and uses, and depending on your strategy—which we will also cover in a later chapter—you will use some and not others.

Before we begin, I also ask you to keep in mind what you learned in the previous chapter: that social media creates the opportunity to not only make but also to broadcast and distribute messages, which means that there may be quite a few more platforms than you might have otherwise thought.

However, each performs these functions in one way or another.

Another thing to keep in mind is that these platforms change. I do not cover in this edition a relative newcomer to the game—Google +. However, I may in the next edition if it becomes more relevant. Likewise, some platforms that I cover here may go away at any time (though I doubt it).

But in either case the fact remains that it is the potential of each platform and not the platform itself that is important, and which you must understand to have a successful social media recruiting strategy.

1. Social Networking Platforms

The first set of platforms we want to look at are known as social networking platforms. These are web-based tools which connect us with others through an open or closed network, and which allow us to share information with those in our network.

Perhaps the one that most people are familiar with is Facebook. With over 800 million users and counting, it is by far the single largest social networking platform in the world.

Chances are you already have an account on Facebook and are somewhat familiar with what it can do and how to use its basic settings.

If you do not have an account yet, please put down this book and go create one, because you will need it in a later chapter.

Through Facebook, users can post pictures, videos, and links to other content and information. They also create status updates, which inform people in their network (their "friends") about what they are doing or how they feel.

In addition they can send each-other email-like messages or instant chat with friends.

Businesses and brands can also create Facebook presences, known as Pages. On these Pages brands can do much of the same as individuals can in their profiles. Brands can share images, videos and information with people who like them and their page (the brand's fans).

Another popular social networking platform is LinkedIn, which has many of the same features and functions as Facebook, but is geared towards a professional group of users.

Through LinkedIn users can share updates, information, and tips. They can ask questions about professionally-related subjects and provide or get referrals from friends or customers. They can also join multiple networks formed to support enthusiasts of specific topics, like marketing or teaching.

Here too brands can start groups or networks for employees or fans of the brand or business.

Aside from these two, the largest two social networking platforms, there are numerous niche platforms, like for example, Ravelry.com, a social network for knitting and crocheting enthusiasts. Lest you think that sites like this are a joke, consider this single site dedicated to this small niche serves 1 million active users!

We will come back to the importance of niche sites in a later chapter.

2. Micro-Blogging

There is really only one platform that I will cover here which falls into this category: Twitter. To many, Twitter is a complete mystery. After all, what can be said in 140 characters and what could anyone say that was at all important enough to follow?

In truth, there is a lot of trivial content on Twitter, and certain brands use it as an advertising platform (which as we will see is the wrong tactic completely), and both of these types of strategies lead to a lack followers as proof that these methods are wrong.

However, other brands are using Twitter to connect to new, potential clients and customers—or in your case, students. They are also using Twitter to keep their brand in front of their current customers and to make them more loyal—potentially referring friends and generally spreading the brand's message.

There are a number of tactics and strategies to use when utilizing Twitter to build your school's brand and spread your message—and we will get to them in a later chapter—but for right now here are the basics.

In Twitter, users follow other users that seem interesting or which have content that they like and find worthwhile. As users gain followers, each can see what the other tweets in the platform's timeline. Interesting content is shared and absorbed, or repackaged and sent to others (a practice known as retweeting—or RT).

The information is distributed and consumed quickly, and does not stay for even the length that Facebook posts stay—but instead disappears quickly.

3. Blogs

Yes, blogs are social media platforms, and perhaps the most powerful available. Why?

Well, think about what we discussed in the last chapter—social media democratizes information distribution and broadcast. Also, it allows people to connect and interact (social communication).

Blogs do just that. Through blogs people create content about any topic they choose and then readers can interact with that information via commenting systems. Oftentimes some of the richest pieces of content in a blog entry are actually found in the comments, where readers provide feedback, more information or otherwise engage with the author, the content, other readers or all three.

And many professional bloggers are known as influencers—their popularity is at a level where what they write influences people to do something, like purchase a product or see a movie, OR go to a certain university or college.

Blogs also generate content that search engines index and rehash, to be found well after it was written by people searching the web for matching information.

Finally, blogs are often connected to other platforms so that the content can be shared across those platforms. Many blog articles or entries have widgets (small pieces of code connecting them to other online mechanisms) that allow the post to be shared via a user's Facebook or Twitter account, bookmarked with a social bookmarking platform, or given a vote-like score for its quality.

Widgets that allow people to share the blog content with other networks, like Twitter, Facebook or Google+.

All of these features combined ensure that blog articles get spread throughout various other platforms to influence even more people.

4. Crowd-Sourcing and Recommendation Communities

Have you ever bought anything online, maybe from Amazon.com or some other online retailer? How did you pick which product you were going to buy? If you are anything like a large portion of the population that shops online, chances are that your decision was at least somewhat influenced by what others said about the product.

The act of evaluating online content, or evaluating real life merchandise or services online, and then merging that evaluation with the evaluations of others, is called crowd-sourcing.

Crowd-sourcing has proven to be one of the most influential drivers of online consumer decision-making.

When a consumer sees two similar products in an online marketplace— again we will just use Amazon.com for familiarity's sake—they will often look at what others have said about those products (in our case, schools) and whether they have provided positive or negative feedback.

Whole communities exist for the purpose of reviewing and evaluating businesses, services and brands. Yelp (www.yelp.com), for example, is an online recommendation community where people evaluate and review everything from plumbers to department stores.

This community in particular is extremely powerful, with a network of millions and over 50 million site visitors every month. Yelp influences numerous decisions about what products and services to purchase and where.

To increase its reach, Yelp and similar communities, also allow users to distribute their content to other networks, like Facebook and Twitter, and further enable media sharing in the form of images and videos.

5. Video and Picture Sharing

Videos and images are two of the most important media for your social presence on the web. They get people talking, get them interested in you and what you do, and demonstrate who you are.

YouTube is probably the biggest and most familiar of the video sharing platforms out there. The web scoring website, Alexa (www.alexa.com), estimates that YouTube receives 450 million site visitors every month! Further, YouTube is ranked as the number two most used search engine following Google, meaning people are turning to YouTube to find information about people, brands businesses and schools.

Add to this the video sharing community and network capacity, as well as the ability to interact with members of that community through comments and feedback, AND the ability to distribute videos and activity to yet other networks, like Facebook, Twitter and LinkedIn, and it is easy to see why YouTube has become one of the most important social media sites there is.

In fact, many experts believe that we are only on the threshold of what is to come in regards to video sharing. This is precisely because videos are so easily made and uploaded, allowing more and more people to do it.

So much so, that experts estimate 48 hours of video are uploaded to YouTube EVERY MINUTE!

YouTube is not the only platform out there, either. There are others like Vimeo (www.vimeo.com) and Yahoo! Video, but YouTube is certainly one of the most critical to understand and use.

Another important set of platforms are image sharing sites, specifically Flickr (www.flickr.com) and Photobucket (www.photobucket.com). Both of these platforms share many of the same characteristics. For example, they both allow users to upload and share images with other users, edit images, and host images for free.

In addition, users join communities and discussion groups with like-minded users, and, as is becoming a common theme, they can share their images with other social networking platforms.

Finally, as with other sites, there is the social quality. Users interact with one another through discussions and comments about one-another's images. They also 'tag' images so that other users are identified in them.

All of this interactivity and feedback is, of course, shareable with/through other networks as well.

Conclusion

As I mentioned earlier, there are many, many other platforms out there, like question-answer communities (where people post questions for the community to answer), forums, wikis, and online gaming communities.

These are all very niche driven areas to focus on. To understand our general and our advanced approaches, though, we will concentrate on a few of the platforms in this chapter.

Action Items

1. Try to think of the niches that your students fall into. Not the students you necessarily want, but the student that you get, those that are on your campus right now. What do they like to do? What are their hobbies? What majors do they primarily go into?

2. Try to find some social networking sites that focus on these niches: sports, gaming, fashion, etc.

3. Of the platforms discussed, which are new to you? Which do you already have a presence on?

4. For those that are new, go to them and create a basic account and start becoming familiar with the platform so that you can begin using them for recruitment purposes later.

4 Last but not Least (Lesser Social Media Platforms)

This chapter explores some of the more obscure but still important social media that you should be aware of. We will only discuss them in brief terms of how you can use them, but your concentration and focus should be on those we investigated in the previous chapter, and in the upcoming four chapters.

1. Social Media 1.0: Forums and Wikis

The term, social media 1.0 was used by Brian Solis in his book Engage, and I thought it was such an appropriate phrase that I unabashedly appropriated it for this one. The 1.0 reference simply denotes that these methods come from a period before we find many of the newest and most popular social media mechanisms. In fact one of these methods—forums—has been around for almost a decade now.

However the term is a bit of a misnomer considering early definitions of Web 2.0 celebrated user-generated content, peer-to-peer interaction, and web-user authorship (among many other characteristics).

We see all three of these characteristics in forums and wikis. In each case it is the users who create the content of the site.

And it is the perhaps the forum that we have to thank for all of the rest of the social media platforms we now enjoy. I do not know one geek who has not haunted the threads of forums to find the answer to some obscure and vague question about the precise problem he or she is having. The forum could be for a Cisco router or for online game, World of Warcraft—forums exist for just about any topic.

Since early 1994 with the introduction of the WWW Interactive Talk project sponsored by the World Wide Web Consortium (the governing body of the internet), internet users have been holding discussions, sharing secrets, having arguments and providing information for one another via forums.

Each forum is typically concentrated on a specific subject, and can generate a number of sub-forums to discuss features or sub-topics of the primary subject. Forum users post comments or questions which are then answered by other forum users.

For some reason, researchers have paid a lot of attention to forums in particular. What they have found is worth noting here. Forum users often create a very real community, albeit an information-based one. This community is self-sustaining, and participating in it takes place whenever users ask questions or respond in the forum (or as some argue, merely in browsing through the threads).

Throughout these forums users are noted with different levels of expertise, sometimes even explicitly labeled with the ranking of "expert" which is displayed close to their name.

As with other forms of social media platforms, the information that users contribute in forums is indexed in search engines and retrieved through internet search queries. What is important to point out is that often, when users enter a question as a search string into a search engine, such as Google, forum topics are found ranked towards the top of the search results.

This is a consequence of similarly structured questions asked within the forum themselves, which leads to a highly accurate return on search queries. So, natural language searching for problem-solutions is becoming an accurate way of finding information due to online forums and all of their content.

The lesson for college recruiting is that if you post information in forums—by asking or answering questions—there is a good chance it will be found by someone. You can also post links to other web pages, which as we will see later is one way of getting articles or videos ranked higher in search engine results.

Forums are good then for peripherally helping to drive traffic to you, but they should not be a center focus.

Another early example of social media is the wiki. Wikis formally debuted (meaning it was the first instance of being called 'wiki') in 1995. Conceptually speaking they are pretty simple: web pages that can be edited within a browser and then saved in addition to all previous pages as historical versions.

The *social* of wikis is in the user content creation. Information found in pages of a wiki is created collaboratively by those reading the wiki. By adding, changing, editing or deleting information, contributors enhance their own understanding about the subject matter and provide other users with more accurate information.

Knowledge on wikis is not so much stacked on top of each other, as in blog comments, but layered, with each new piece of information taking the place of old, vague or inaccurate information.

Missing is the discussion between and amongst contributors, allowing users to judge for themselves who may be most accurate. Wiki histories, however, allow us to see the evolution of pages: what people have added or changed in the time of the page's existence. We can see how knowledge is refined, expanded and honed, leaving users with accurate information.

For our purposes here, understand that like forums you can contribute to wikis and help create knowledge about areas within your expertise—like about your school or the college admission process. As is the case with forums, they are good avenues to drive traffic.

You will also see in a later chapter that monitoring what is said by others on social media sites is important. Wikis are certainly included in that instruction, especially specific wiki entries pertaining to your school (like Wikipedia's entry, for example).

2. You've Got Questions…Quora et al.

One of the things that forums excel at is getting your questions answered or providing solutions to your problems. However it is sometimes difficult to get this accomplished.

Most forums have rules and guidelines to follow before you post to them, and then further procedures and standards to follow when you do post. A noted downside of using forums is that information may be slow in coming or inaccurate when it does come. And God help you if you ever post a question in the wrong section.

Enter the Q&A site. There are a number of them throughout the internet, such as Yahoo! Answers (http://answers.yahoo.com), Answers.com (http://wiki.answers.com), and Askville by Amazon.com (http://askville.amazon.com). Each of these mechanisms is fairly similar in that they are focused on question and answer formats. Content is generated by members of the community and the answers given are rated by registered users (as are the members answering the questions) and all content is indexed, searchable and found via online searches.

There is no limit to the types of questions people can ask: everything from politics to economics, gaming and everything in between is fair game. Moderators are present, and both questions and answers are policed for tastefulness and appropriateness (for the most part, though, these tools are crowd-sourced—depending on the mass of users to police and moderate them).

At first glance these mechanisms certainly check the "social" box of social media—meaning that information is created and distributed by users alone—but they do not seem as "networky" as some of the previous mechanisms—meaning they don't seem to connect people like Facebook or Twitter.

However, upon deeper investigation these mechanisms are quite networked, and members become part of large communities within them, even importing their profiles and personas from other mechanisms.

For example, because it is part of the Yahoo! Network, Flickr users have the same username in Yahoo! Answers, both when asking or answering a question. The result affects their persona within Yahoo! Answers, but that persona is also linked to the persona within Flickr as well—if their answers are rated low in one, it affects the other.

The same is true for Askville: users of that utility are members of the vast Amazon network, which is very active in exchanging information through ratings and comments aimed at both brands and products.

A relatively new site that vastly extends the social networking functionality—and truly by extension the social media functionality—is Quora (http://www.quora.com). Quora links the Q&A functionality of other sites to the users' personas on Facebook or Twitter.

While most other Q&A sites will send you email notifications when someone asks or answers questions—especially if you are involved in the conversation—Quora posts it to your Facebook status or sends a tweet for each question you ask or answer you give.

Quora users can additionally follow other users and then also get notified when they ask or answer questions. Answers are also sorted and rated and can themselves be commented on further, expanding the content within each conversation. Finally, another helpful feature is that answers are searched and retrieved in online searches.

The upshot of this type of social media is that it is very specifically designed to put people in front of the answers they seek. The answers, most importantly, are created by other users—brands are not involved (other than the mechanisms themselves).

In the case of Quora, it adds a very specific dimension to an already overwhelming slew of social networking functions. The bottom line is that information is more precisely matched with the users who need it.

These are important sites for you to monitor (as we will discuss later), but not to focus on. Through searches you will run into questions asked that you can and should answer, specifically questions about your school, the admission process, etc.

3. Dude, where's my…? Location-based Social Media

The pervasiveness of smart-phones and geo-synching technology has enabled the growth of social media tools and mechanisms that coordinate a user's position with some type of user-generated data. In some instances the utility is itself a mechanism within another social media, like the Check-in feature in Facebook.

This feature synchs a smart-phone's coordinates with businesses at those coordinates. It then displays that information on your Facebook status as "USER just checked in at LOCATION." Of course, as with most other applications on Facebook, users can "tag" their friends (list people they know at the location as well) and comment on their status.

One social media mechanism that completely focuses on location-based social media is Foursquare (http://www.foursquare.com). In terms of its functionality it works almost exactly like the Facebook check-in function—in fact users can connect their Foursquare and

Facebook accounts and display their Foursquare check-ins on Facebook.

Because it solely focuses on location-based content, the creators of Foursquare have explored many more features and functions, like treasure-hunt style games, or contests for location check-ins (i.e. who checks in the most times at any given place).

What becomes of that information can be up to the location in question or up to other users. Important to note is that this information is shared over a number of different networks and uses a multitude of media. The information is also created by the users—either those who are checking-in to a location or those at the location (for example, a bar that offers specials to those who check-in). Locations, thus, have become social (if they weren't already).

For the purposes of admission, it would be important to ensure that each building on campus, if possible, has a presence on Foursquare. As with other mechanisms, your brand is shared when a user checks in to your brand. So when a potential student checks in to your school's library on a tour, her friends will see this check in. As we will see, the influence of others through social media is a huge and important factor for your success.

Action Items

1. Go to Foursquare.com and see how many buildings at your school are listed in the website.
2. Create a place for any that are not already there
3. Go to Quora.com or other Q&A site and search your school's name. Do any questions come up?

4. Are there any forums that exist that are about your school? How about any that focus on college admissions. Are there any threads you could or should comment on?

5 Who's Using Social Media (and what are they doing)?

In the past decade, the use of social media has grown steadily across all sectors, industries, cultures, ages—practically all demographics.

As a communication tool, social media has grown from blogs and earlier mechanisms, like forums and bulletin boards, to much more dynamic and interactive platforms.

At the same time, some platforms that were particularly strong and looked to be THE platform to use quickly faded away.

Here we are going to look at the use of social media by organizations, including both corporations and universities, and by the end user—with particular attention paid to the major demographic we are interested in: high school-aged, primarily U.S.-based students.

1. Corporations and Businesses Using Social Media

In 2010, Pepsi Corp, decided to forgo spending its money on a Super Bowl ad, and instead invested 20 million dollars into a social media marketing campaign (3).

Pepsi was ahead of the curve in 2010. Everyone wondered how useful it would be to really initiate a full social media marketing campaign, and further we were struggling to figure out how to do it in the first place.

This has changed, though, and businesses and brands all over the world are scrambling to learn and use social media platforms to extend their messages. It is no longer a question of "if" they should use social media: they know they need to use it. The trick now is to understand where to create a presence for the particular audience.

According to a 2011 study sponsored by the marketing-based blog site, Social Media Examiner, 92% of marketing professionals select Facebook as the most important social media platform for marketing.

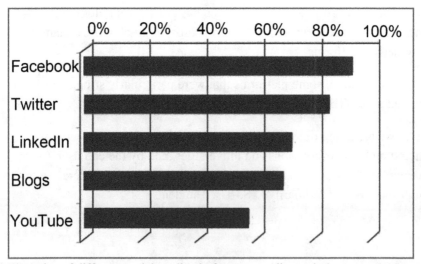

The value of different social media platforms according to industry marketing professionals (2011).

The following four rounded out the top five most important platforms:

- Twitter: 84%
- LinkedIn: 71%
- Blogs: 68%
- YouTube: 56% (4)

These are, of course, averages across all industries and business sizes. Remember that just like in other aspects in life, there is no one-size-fits all approach. We will examine your school's strategy in a later chapter, but know that at the very least these five are deemed the most important by industry and corporations.

And the trends suggest the focus on social media will not decrease. According to a report by Forbes, spending on "interactive media" will rise to $77 billion dollars by 2016—26% of the total spent on marketing by all organizations (5).

Social media makes up one of the largest components in the "interactive media" category.

And according to Bonsai Interactive, large businesses are already spending a lot of money on their social media strategy and campaigns. Their 2010 study found that the average large organization is spending over $210,000 a year (6).

What is more, according to an Altimeter Group report, enterprise-level businesses spent $833,000.00 on social media marketing and strategy in 2010. This number was expected to rise dramatically for 2011 (7).

A 2010 Syncapse study argues that the reward reaped by these businesses is measured as being much higher than what they spend. The rewards are also distributed across a number of segments, including (in order of importance):

- Customer engagement
- Direct customer communication
- Speed of feedback
- Learning customer's preferences
- Brand building
- Market research
- Reach
- Lead generation
- Customer service (8).

Another study released in 2011 by the email marketing company, Constant Contact, found that of the businesses they studied, 96% had presences on Facebook. Of these, 86% counted this marketing platform as effective (9).

The same company, in a different study, found that in late 2011, 81% of small businesses reported using social media in their marketing strategy. The same study found that social media use is rapidly on the rise by these small businesses. Their survey conducted in the spring of 2011 stated that only 76% of the same small businesses used social media (10).

That is a 5% increase in only three or four months!

The bottom line is that social media as a platform for marketing by organizations, including universities and colleges, is no longer in question. It is valid and it is utterly important.

At the very least, you MUST have the same focus as your competitors.

But, the most optimum approach is to go where your customers are. That is the next element we will look at.

2. Social Media Use by Consumers

So how often are social media platforms used, and by whom?

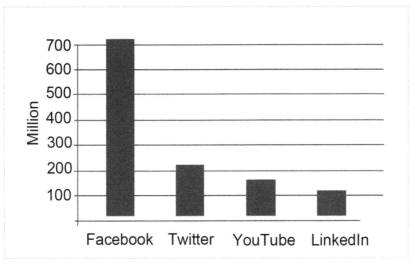

Number of unique visits/month to the major social media sites (2011).

According to late November 2011 statistics reported by the web traffic recording site, Alexa, the social media sites used most often are:

Facebook—700 million unique visitors every month

Twitter—200 million unique visitors every month

YouTube—142 million unique visitors every month

LinkedIn—100 million unique visitors every month

These statistics are mind-boggling, especially when you consider that these rankings do not take into account the views received for embedded media—like YouTube movies embedded in other websites that are viewed but not recorded as a unique visit to YouTube itself.

The same goes for Facebook and Twitter conversations that stream the platform's interface through a different site or mechanism (called a client).

Also notice that blogs are not included here, simply because there is no single blog platform like there are different social media platforms.

Instead blogs are spread throughout the internet on individual websites or blog sites.

However, according to one of the most popular blogging mechanisms (which is hosted on other sites), called WordPress, there are as of November 2011 over 66 million blogs around the world using this single platform. Further, its statistics claim that WordPress blogs are read by over 321 million people each month.

Again, what remarkable statistics. Every month an online population almost the size of the population of the United States reads online blog articles. So surely, this platform would rank blogs as one of the top five social media platforms to use.

Each of these platforms additionally boasts huge numbers of members.

Facebook is currently well over 800 million users worldwide.

Twitter, once very niche and used by a small number, had as of March 2011 over 175 million users.

YouTube currently hosts over 50 million registered users, which is a fraction of the traffic they see mainly from non-registered viewers.

LinkedIn finally broke the 100 million mark in mid-2011, ranking them in the top five for number of registered participants in its community.

Users also spend an enormous amount of time on these platforms. Every Facebook user, according to their 2011 statistics, spends over 15 hours a month on the site. And every month, online users spend 2.9 billion hours watching YouTube videos.

30 billion pieces of content—pictures, videos, files and posts—are shared on Facebook monthly. 190 million messages—or tweets—are sent daily on Twitter. 3000 images are uploaded to Flickr every minute. And YouTube gets 48 hours of new video every minute.

The lesson is that social media is where people are spending their time. They are sharing information with each other every second, and these platforms have become integrated into their daily lives.

So what do they do when they go to these places? What are they actually saying to each-other on Facebook or Twitter?

According to yet another Nielsen survey, 89% of people on social media are primarily using it to connect to friends, relatives and loved ones (11).

When it comes to brands and businesses—like your school—people are not logging in to the platforms specifically to find out about you, instead they are logging in to see what others have to say about you.

Remember in the previous chapter we talked about word-of-mouth and how important recommendations from other consumers are? This is where the lessons really begin to connect. In other words, people want to know about you, so they log into Facebook or Twitter and search for conversations about you.

What are the bottom line take-aways? Well, there are two issues to understand:

1. There has to be conversation about you in the first place to make you relevant.
2. The conversation should be positive.

Ultimately you must ensure conversations are taking place, and you must lead the conversations in a positive direction to influence those people who want to know about you.

Okay, so we know where people are going to use social media, what platforms they are one, and how they are using those platforms.

Now we need to better understand where *your* demographic may be. We are going to now look at where users in the 14+ age group are spending time.

41

According to a 2010 Pew Research Center study, 73% of online teens use social networking. This is the second biggest group of online users, just behind the 18-29 year old demographic at 82% (12).

Of the most popular sites, Facebook was by far the social network they spent the most amount of time.

This is actually true for all it seems. Of online users 12 and older, 51% use Facebook! And while the largest number of Facebook users falls in the 18-24 year old camp (30%) according to a 2010 study, the third largest number of Facebook users (15%) are found in the 13-17 year old age range (13).

YouTube was the second most used social media site visited by this group of teenagers. Twitter usage was much lower. Only about 11% of teenagers have Twitter accounts, but what is important about this is that they are mainly using it to "listen."

In other words, instead of having conversations on Twitter, they are watching other conversations taking place and absorbing what is going on.

In general members of this demographic are trading "social objects" (pictures, videos), sharing news and information, and connecting with friends and family.

According to Facebook, users are interacting with 900 million objects on the site. Consider that 15% of Facebook users are in the 13-17 year old age group, which creates a pool of 135 million objects shared, traded and viewed by your potential students.

Further, this group of teenagers is increasingly using Facebook to communicate with friends. According to a Pew Research Center poll conducted in 2010, the number of teenagers using Facebook to message in 2009 was 21%. That number climbed to 25% in 2010, and seems to be steadily rising (14).

In general, the most often cited reason for using social media for all demographics was to *connect*—specifically to connect with friends and family.

A 2011 IBM study reported that over 70% of social media users are on networking sites to keep in touch with and communicate with those they know and love (15).

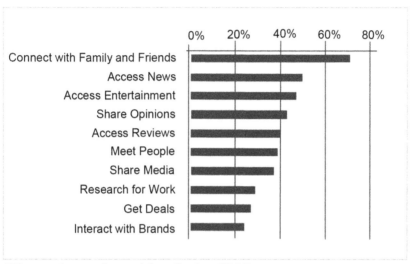

Why people are using social media sites (2011).

Other important reasons included in the findings are the following:

- Share opinion (42%)
- Access Reviews (39%)
- Interact with Brands (23%)

We can draw some pretty important conclusions from all of these statistics and variables.

First, they tell us that the demographic you are interested in, 13-17 year olds, *are* using social media—a lot! It also tells us that of all the social media platforms you need to use, Facebook, YouTube and Twitter are the most important when trying to market to potential college students.

LinkedIn, MySpace, and other networks will be important, but the biggest lakes to cast nets into are the three most often used.

Another take away is in knowing that they are not going to social media platforms to interact with brands or to be advertised to.

On the surface that sounds a bit discouraging. I mean, is that not the whole point for you and your school?

However, look beyond this finding and at the other ones.

We know potential students are looking at what others say about the schools they are interested in. Knowing this emphasizes the importance of monitoring what is being said and engaging with those who have questions (we will cover this later).

We also know they share opinions about…everything. From products to music to universities, they are informing others about how they feel and what they know about brands and businesses.

Again it will be important to monitor social media platforms to see what is being said about you, and at the very least to understand what you can do better. Perhaps even more important though is that this statistic should really provide the impetus to start engaging with potential students, instead of just sitting back and watching them engage each other about you!

I know you are asking yourself, "How do we do that?"

Especially considering the last statistic provided: only 23% of social media users interact with brands.

What do they do? Where do they go? Who do they talk to?

Every case is going to be different. The students that go to the small technical college in Tennessee are different than the students who go to the city university. They will read different things, use different platforms, and follow different people.

The goal is for you to understand your users, and then go get them. We will look at how to do that in just a few chapters!

Action Items

1. Go to http://search.twitter.com and enter the name of your school in the search box. What do you find? What is being said about you? That is the conversation being "listened to" by your audience on Twitter.

2. Look at your biggest competitor or competitors. What platforms are they using?

3. Look at their pages and Twitter feeds. What are they saying? How often are they posting? Are people interacting with them?

6 How Social Media Ties into Marketing

In this chapter we will look at how social media differs from traditional marketing, advertising and public relations (PR). We will need this understanding to clear out old ideas and make way for the new methods and strategies demanded by social media.

One of the most daunting things that businesses and organizations face is getting past the traditional marketing paradigms.

Marketing and advertising are business tools most any professional is very familiar with. And why not? We have been using the same approaches for decades. Television advertising, print and billboards—these are things we have grown up with and know and understand.

We also understand marketing campaigns. When a product or service is rolled out we create a campaign to generate interest and push the product or service. The objective is to create buzz and get people to buy. Easy, right?

We know and are familiar with this type of approach to advertising and marketing. It is comfortable to us and it is kind of hard to leave things that are comfortable.

So, naturally, when universities and colleges start looking at how they can use social media to help their recruiting effort, they try to apply the old methods of marketing and advertising they understand.

But social media demands that we change the way we approach advertising or marketing. Remember that social media is a form of communication, not just a tool for communicating. As such we need to figure out the communication strategies, not marketing strategies to use.

To simplify things, I have come up with a list of five ways that social media marketing differs from traditional marketing.

These five ways are:

1. Social media marketing is a permission-based platform.
2. Social media marketing depends on word-of-mouth.
3. Social media marketing is personal and individualized.
4. Social media marketing focuses on the niches.
5. Social media marketing is about listening.

The rest of this chapter elaborates on these differences. The hope is that by the end of it, you will understand why you need to let go of old methods and embrace new ones. Once you understand these differences, we will then look at specific tactics and strategies to follow.

1. Social Media Marketing is a Permission-Based Platform

Traditional marketing tools rely on interruption to broadcast a message.

Think about it for a moment.

Television commercials interrupt the actual program. Newspaper advertisements interrupt our reading. Billboards interrupt our view.

All of this is carried out in attempt to make consumers pay attention to something. Thus, what consumers want to do is interrupted by what an advertiser wants to tell them. You can see why consumers do not really like advertisements.

Another way of looking at it is that traditional advertising pushes its message on you, like some sloppy drunk at a bar.

It says, "Here's my product! Buy it"

The natural response for most consumers is to ignore it.

And in the past 20 years that type of advertising has drastically lost its effectiveness. In a recent study of television viewers who watched programs interrupted by commercials, only 15% could recall the subject of the commercials they viewed one week later.

Considering television ads are the most costly form of advertising, it amounts to a colossal waste of money when 85% of the target audience does not even remember what you were advertising, let alone your brand or the details.

The historical view has been to simply say, "Well we need to keep our brand name in front of people all of the time to ensure recognition and recall." How many ad spots would it take to ensure this?

But social media runs completely counter to the interrupt-and-push methods of advertising.

For starters, marketing through social media relies on someone's permission to market to them.

This is true for every platform we use, from Facebook to blogs.

In the case of a platform like Facebook, users have to choose to 'Like' your university's page before you can start talking to them—literally they have to opt-in to see your message. And at any given moment, they can opt-out of your message by 'un-liking' you just as easily.

And once they are gone, it is very difficult to get them back.

The case is true for all other platforms as well. For example, if they come to your site to read your blog, they do so by choice. The same goes for videos on YouTube. It is demonstrated even more by their decision to subscribe to your blog or YouTube Channel—that is permission to give them even more.

And when it comes to network-based programs like Twitter or LinkedIn, they must also give you their permission to talk to them.

The permission they give is based on their interest to get to know you and your school.

Unfortunately, so many people, still used to the old habits, want to then pounce on these students and bombard them with ad-based messages like, "why you should go to school here," or "why a degree from our school is more valuable."

All tactics like these do is turn off the potential students and force them to 'unlike' you again.

And who could blame them?

Imagine signing up for a cable network only to find nothing but channels dedicated to commercials. How long would it take you to unsubscribe from that network?

Instead of pushing your message onto potential students, you need to allow them to pull it willingly towards themselves.

In other words, you need them to first give you permission to market to them. They do this by liking you on Facebook, following you on Twitter, searching out and reading your blog entries, subscribing to and viewing your YouTube videos.

Once they have given you permission, then you need them to pull your message willingly. They need to want to see what you have to say. They need to be interested in your content enough to look forward to reading it.

2. Social Media Campaigns Depend on Word of Mouth

Who do you trust more, a car salesman or your best friend? I mean no offense to car salesmen, of course, but we all trust our best friend more, especially when it comes to giving us a recommendation about which car to buy.

The car salesman is going to tell us the best car we can buy is one he sells. Our best friend, though, will give us an honest answer.

Word of mouth and trust in the person providing recommendations are elements that drastically separate traditional marketing and advertising from social media marketing.

Traditional marketing and advertising relies on the organization—your university—to broadcast its own message of value and worth.

In other words, you tell people why you are so wonderful.

This is the model followed by just about every business and organization around the world.

"Buy this car because it is the best!"

"Eat at this restaurant because it will make you more handsome"

"Go to our school because you will get a better job, have more fun, enjoy your classes…"

So how trustworthy is this method? Do people really care what you have to say about your school? More importantly, do they actually trust what YOU are saying about your school?

According to a 2009 Nielsen survey study, while between 24-70% of people trust what organizations have to say about themselves, their brands or products (depending on the advertising method used), 90% of people trust the opinions of their friends. 90%! (16).

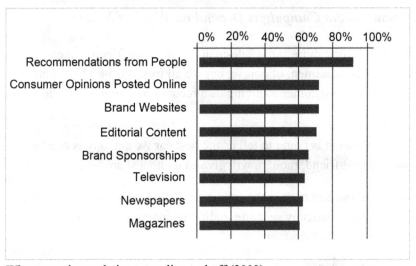

Where people put their trust online and off (2009).

Imagine in our climate how important this statistic is. When someone on Facebook posts their opinion, feedback or criticism about your university, they and their opinion is trusted more than anything you could possibly say to potential students.

And while word-of-mouth has probably always had this impact, the potential to broadcast it to thousands of people has only become available through social media networks.

Here is what I mean.

Let us say I have 250 friends on Facebook. I write a post offering my opinion about your school—maybe my desire to go there. 250 people see it. Maybe 10 of those people provide some type of feedback on my post—perhaps they "like" it or they write a comment about it.

Everybody they are friends with sees the feedback they provide.

So now let us imagine those 10 people average 200 friends each. That is 2000 people, plus the original 250 who have now potentially seen the opinions I have about your school.

If it is the right opinion, then it is terrifically valuable and free marketing performed on your behalf but without any cost, AND the possible outcome is a more trustworthy and valued message than anything you could ever create and distribute in the first place.

Other networks have even more potential, like Twitter or LinkedIn. Videos or blog articles that friends write could also potentially reach hundreds of future students.

Further, the survey by Nielsen said that at most, the highest number that anyone will ever trust your message is about 70%. And that number is limited to only one mechanism: your website.

However, all online opinions by others not associated with your university is trusted by at least that much, regardless of the method it is broadcast in.

Think of the scope of forms these messages can take: videos, blogs, comments on blogs, forum messages and posts, Facebook posts, tweets on Twitter, ratings and reviews on various sites across the internet.

The bottom line is that word-of-mouth marketing is the most powerful mechanism available to us right now.

Further, the model of advertising that puts the university at the center of the message—the creator and broadcaster, so to speak—is becoming more and more irrelevant when compared to the information future students are receiving from other people (called, third parties) through social media.

3. Social Media is Personal and Individual

In traditional advertising and marketing the technique is typically to broadcast a message to as many people as you might assume are in your target demographic or audience.

Universities spend a lot of money on these traditional admission and recruiting tactics. Paper brochures and marketing materials, attending high school college fairs across the country, television and print advertisements, etc.

These methods add up to an enormous amount of time and resources dedicated to antiquated strategies.

The idea is to cast as big of a net as possible to catch the most fish. The problem, though, is that the number of lakes have grown in quantity but reduced in actual size.

What I mean is that there are now so many potential places to "fish," these strategies just do not work anymore.

Let us face it, how many college fairs can you or your counselors go to before the costs simply outweigh the potential number of students.

At one time these types of advertising and marketing campaigns made sense. After all, when people only had three television channels to choose from, it was a safe bet that if we placed our ads on all three—during the programs our customers would most likely watch—we would get at least some customers in return.

And even now this strategy kind of makes sense. Though customers have numerous TV channels to view, they are so segmented by topic and interest that one might think it would actually be a good thing.

But consider this. According to a Nielsen study from 2009, 59% of Americans simultaneously watch TV and surf the internet (17). That number has surely risen as well.

In other words, the attention of consumers has been shattered. Attempting to reach as many as possible through the "wide-net" approach (or the shotgun approach as some call it), results in an even lower payback than before.

The answer, then, is to get personal. Stop trying to appeal to crowds and instead appeal to individuals.

That is what social media marketing attempts to do: it focuses on one person at a time. This is carried out in a number of ways, but especially through conversations and attention to single potential students.

This is nothing new for admissions counselors. In fact, individual focus has been at the heart of university and college-level student recruitment since it became a profession. However, social media platforms, combined with the unique mechanisms of social media (like the permission-based concept), take the individual focus to an entirely new level, and create new possibilities.

Now admissions counselors can reach out to future students in their own networks, and can provide advice and answer questions on a scale and level that they could only dreamed about five years ago.

Social media marketing is about selling yourself to the individual: *that* is what will provide you with new students. If you try to appeal to them as a crowd, they will instead go to the school that appreciates them in a one-on-one, individual relationship.

4. *Social Media Marketing Focuses on Niches*

After learning principle number 3, "Social Media is Personal and Individual," many people ask, "If it is about focusing on the single, individual student, where do we find him/her?"

Good question. Social media gives us the ability to segment our customers (potential students) into very fine shards, unlike traditional marketing tools that simply group them together.

Once again I will pick on TV ads to demonstrate what I mean. Traditional advertising can narrow an audience down to very large segments based on surface-level demographics as the primary characteristics. Aspects like age, income and education level, and geographic locales help a little bit, but far too little.

It helps a bit to know things like interests, music preference, favorite sports teams and food tastes, but again this still breaks people out into rather large segments. One benefit of the multitude of cable channels and saturated programming is that you can advertise to audiences of shows with particular topics or focus, like Italian cooking or baseball.

But still, you spend massive amounts of money to throw your message at a large group that may or may not want to hear it.

Instead, by using social media, we can target our message to individual members of niche groups we find online.

Try to search for the oddest topic you can that at least a few of your students might be interested in. How about marching band competitions? How many groups and communities do you find? Oftentimes you can even narrow these niches down further into geographic locations and importance.

The most obvious example of this is found in the Facebook advertising platform. Because users willingly give Facebook so much information about themselves, advertisers can very precisely micro-target ads and messages just for a very small group of potential students.

You could seek out and find, for example, students interested in your particular sports teams, like maybe your basketball team (if you have one). Then you can create niche messages just for those potential students. Next, you could find potential students interested in one of the particular, popular degrees you offer, and then again tailor your message specifically for that niche.

The number of topics and number of niches are almost limitless.

Your job will be to find them and begin participating in them (we will discuss how later).

5. Social Media Marketing is About Listening

Traditional marketing is about broadcasting. It is a one-way transmission of the message from the business to the customer.

In this model there is no interaction, no feedback or conversation.

In fact, feedback may occur before the broadcast in the form of focus groups, where "model" customers view and provide feedback about the message. But once the message is sent, there is no loop that compensates for what the customer has to say after they have listened to the message.

More than that, this model does not account for what the customer might actually want. Though surveys could demonstrate what a percentage of a large group likes or desires, it dismisses—once again—individuals.

So instead of talking with people and trying to understand how to help them, traditional advertising and marketing pushes the message (once more) onto them, lumps them all together into large groups, and then ignores anything they have to say.

Is it any wonder that as soon as a mechanism came out to actually interact, people jumped on it and stopped listening to businesses that continued to simply shout at them?

Social media provides the means to actually listen to potential students, not just hear them (which is the case with surveys and focus groups).

You can now actually listen to their concerns and worries, wants and desires.

The information gleaned from listening becomes the ammunition in your arsenal. You understand now what it will take for students to come to your school, to learn more about your financial aid, or to tour your campus.

What a wonderful concept! Whereas before we could not hear or listen to the potential students because we were too busy talking, we can now sit back and let them tell us how to get them into our school!

Listening is not easy, however—and in fact, listening is perhaps a bad way of putting it because it implies that it is the only method. Perhaps learning is a better word.

And there are dozens of ways we can learn about potential students.

We can learn about them through the videos they post and watch. By the pictures they share. In the information they comment on or like. By what their profiles and friends' profiles say. Or by the networks they join.

Each of these social objects (as we will call them) offers a small amount of information that helps define the person. As we look more and more at these objects, we build a better understanding about the potential student (remember, we are doing this individually) and what it is he or she cares about, wants or needs.

Conclusion

All of these items work in unison or feed into the other. We treat potential students as individuals that we listen to and learn about. We interact with them in the niches they belong to and we gain permission to talk to them. Through word of mouth they spread our message for us, and then their friends, followers, and people in their networks begin talking to us and allowing us to share our message.

The community you create grows exponentially as more and more begin choosing you as a resource.

Ultimately, through social media, you cultivate and grow a population of very dedicated community members who want to go to your school and experience all you have been teaching them about.

Now that we understand there are differences between social media and traditional marketing and advertising, we can move onto the goals of engagement through social media.

Action Items

1. Write down every form of advertising your school currently uses—everything: from billboards to viewbooks. How many of them are geared to groups versus small segments?

2. Look at your current advertising again. How many of your advertising mechanisms are interruptive or use the push methods? Are there any that use permission-based methods?

3. How many of them provide some type of feedback or interaction loop so that potential students can easily talk to you?

4. Go online and search for some niche communities that your students might belong to. What do you find? Are there any you cannot find communities for?

7 Goals for Social Media Marketing

We will spend this chapter looking at the actual goals to set for a social media marketing campaign.

At first it seems odd that we would even consider the question. The obvious answer should be: we want to increase enrollment. And like any campaign this will require a number of other sub-goals, like reaching our target demographic, creating higher brand awareness, etc.

Marketing through social media will do all of that, of course, but what makes the new approach different is that it does it over time and through engagement.

While our primary goal—increasing enrollment—remains the same, we need to understand a number of new and important sub-goals that you may have never had to worry about before.

Specifically, we need to understand the importance of:

- Audience size
- Audience quality
- Engagement frequency
- Engagement quality

- Audience engagement focus

We will focus on these five sub-goals for the rest of this chapter for the purpose of developing a complete understanding about our campaign's goal—what we want to do and accomplish by using social media to recruit potential students.

1. Audience Size (Goal: Create a large audience of fans, followers and friends)

This is perhaps the first and foremost goal of most people working in social media. The popular thought is that the larger the audience, the more successful the campaign. And to a point this is true.

And in fact there are a number of companies that prey on businesses and organizations that believe this. For a couple of thousand dollars you could get tens of thousands of followers in a matter of weeks.

But this is not the point.

We *should* try to get a large audience. After all we are talking about a group of people who want to hear from us, who want to see our name in front of them, and who will potentially become students.

But what if they do not really want to go to school at your university? Sure, they enjoy hearing from you, but so what? Does it really do any good to spend time chasing and engaging people who may never enroll?

And this is the point that is entirely missed when we simply pursue numbers—more Twitter followers, more Facebook likes, more LinkedIn connections, etc.

On a side note, because this is such an easy measurement this is often what typifies the return on investment calculation in many places, but do not let it become yours (we will look closely at ROI in a later chapter).

So what we should strive for is a large audience, yes, but it should also be an audience of quality.

2. Audience Quality (Goal: Fill your social media audience with people who will actually convert—enroll or cause others to enroll)

What is your ideal potential student? What does that person's parents look like? Who does that person listen to and trust?

These are the people you must try to reach, because these are the people that may actually either enroll, or influence someone else to enroll.

Your audience size then is in direct proportion to your audience quality. And the only way to know if your audience is the quality you are looking for is to research where they may be and to find ways to attract them to your brand.

There is an important point to make here that is related to a point made earlier: people trust the opinions of friends and relatives more than anyone else. With this in mind it may not be enough to only engage with potential students. Instead go for an even higher quality of audience by influencing the potential student's parents and friends.

When the conversation includes their opinions, and their opinions are favorable, the potential student will more likely trust your brand, be willing to engage you, and hopefully go to your school.

3. Engagement frequency (Goal: Create engagement opportunities with your audience)

Engagement is the term used for the collective interactions you have with audiences. These take on a number of different forms depending on the platform. In Facebook it could be a comment to a status post, a like, or a share (so called when someone 'shares' your post with their friends).

On Twitter this could mean a retweet, reply or mention. On YouTube and on blogs it could mean shares or comments.

The point is that somehow your audience is interacting with the message you are providing. They are, in other words, engaging you.

When it comes to social media, engagement means a great deal. It means that the message you are providing is interesting and relevant to the people you are targeting. Not only do they care enough to respond, but they also care enough to perhaps distribute the message to others.

When your followers become the people sharing your message, you are creating a network of referrals about you and your school. And as we have seen already, people trust messages from other people more than they trust them from you.

So, frequent engagement from quality audiences is perhaps one of the most important factors of success we can pursue.

4. Engagement quality (Goal: Create high-quality engagements with audiences)

Not only should frequent engagement be a goal, but high-quality engagement should also be sought after.

You do not only want your audience to engage through likes and retweets, you want them to hold conversations with you, ask you questions, offer suggestion and insights.

Remember that many people are not interacting, but instead staying in the background and watching and listening to everyone else. The conversations you have with a few followers, the questions you answer, and the back-and-forth dialogues that go on in these types of interactions, are followed closely by others.

Combine this with the fact that consumers trust what others say about a brand more often than what the brand has to say about itself, and you can see the necessity for really trying to engage your audience.

Look for opportunities to simply talk to people. Reply to mentions on Twitter (which we will cover later), thank people for retweeting you, answer questions on Facebook and elsewhere, and comment on the comments that other people leave.

This is time-consuming, no doubt, but it is also the most valuable aspect of social media for businesses in the first place. Without this interaction, social media would be no different than other one-sided forms of communication that consumers have become bored and annoyed with. And if this happens, you are back to square one.

5. Audience engagement focus (Goal: Create a consistent focus on what you say and do)

The repeatability of audience engagement is extremely important, but it is an aspect that few others have really talked about.

Even if you are getting a high number of consumer engagement episodes, how frequently from the same people? Are they random or does it seem like there is a dedicated group of very loyal followers that not only respond to your every post, but also share these with others.

This type of consistency is the focus of your audience. If an audience is very focused on you and your message, you will quickly see that posts are being engaged by the same people on a regular basis.

This is so important and valuable when it occurs. It indicates that when necessary you can count on posts being distributed by a dedicated group, and can begin to include their network in your measurements (such as audience reach and potential size of audience).

These people will almost certainly respond to pleas for help, such as when you might need assistance getting an important message out.

These people are won over by consistent, high-quality engagement. They will evangelize your word, and if they do not plan on going to your school they will almost certainly recommend you.

Conclusion

As we move along you will learn more about taking steps to accomplish these sub-goals. What is important to understand now is that each must be included in a strategy, because otherwise you are trying to hit goals that are not practical for social media.

By setting these sub-goals you create a realistic outcome for yourself and your school.

Action Items

1. Go look at the Facebook page of a brand or company that you like.

2. How many times do they engage their audience?

3. How many people leave comments and like posts in comparison to the size of the audience that actually 'likes' the page?

4. Does it seem that they care about their audience? What do their posts look like? Do they mainly talk about themselves or do they talk about other topics more often?

8 How to *Un-market*

As we have already covered, marketing through social media is not the explicit type of advertising you may be used to. Instead it is a form of personal engagement intended to keep your name in front of the potential students who actually want you to talk to them.

This type of approach is sometimes called, un-marketing. The phrase emphasizes the point that marketing through social media is different in just about every way from traditional marketing.

For example, traditional marketing pushes its message on people by interrupting them. The objective of social media marketing, on the other hand, is to be invited to talk about your school.

But how do you do this?

This is the single most confusing—or confounding—aspect, and it is the point that so very few people get.

To do this, to un-market, you must give people information that they want to receive.

Sounds a bit too simplistic, I know. It is worth really focusing on this however.

People go online for two reasons: to be entertained or to be educated. That is what you must do: educate and/or entertain them.

Your status posts and tweets should share information that your potential audience would find interesting and relevant. This information could be tangentially related to your school, but most importantly it is related to your audience.

From the outside looking in, it might seem odd that you are not spending your time talking about your school—about how wonderful it is, about the size of classes, about the quality of the faculty—but if you were to do that, you would not have an audience. Remember, social media is not an advertising medium, and talking about yourself is nothing more than advertising.

I will give you an example of what I mean.

The New Mexico Institute of Mining and Technology—where I directed the social media strategies—is a very small, very specialized research university in the small town of Socorro, New Mexico. The student population is small, but composed of very smart, very technical students interested in things like science-fiction, online and computer gaming, and science and technology.

To relate to the audience of current, past and potential students on the school's Facebook Page, we shared a consistent stream of posts related to video game systems, zombie movies, computers and scientific discoveries.

The posts are thoughtful or interesting, like articles shared from Wired magazine (http://www.wired.com), or funny and entertaining, like a cartoon from PhD Comics.

Importantly, these posts always create interaction between the current, past and future students. In fact, engagement regularly occurs between and amongst them, and between them and the page administrators.

While sharing content that fits the interests of their audience, the administrators also weave in stories about the school written by others—for example, a report by US News that ranks the school highly. They will also share news and information written by others about the school's faculty, programs, research, accomplishments, etc.

Now while this may seem to run counter to what I said before about not talking about yourself, it actually is quite acceptable, primarily because they are sharing what others have said instead of saying it themselves.

Lastly, they also use the page to post general information—news stories written by the public information office, dates and upcoming events, and important deadlines to potential and current students.

So while they do occasionally focus on themselves, their audience forgives them because of the other entertaining or thoughtful information they provide.

This is the approach that should be taken throughout the array of social media channels you use, from Facebook to Twitter. To make it easy, simply remember these key points:

- Share information that educates your audience
- Share information that makes your audience laugh
- Share information your audience wants
- Do not talk about yourself, but share what others say about you

In order to do this right, you must understand two things: what your audience wants to hear about, and where to find information to share. The remainder of this chapter will address these two very important points.

1. What does your Audience Want to Hear?

This is actually a very easy question to answer, depending on how much you know about your audience. Simply identify who they are and what their interests might be to understand the type of content to provide.

To help you can build a profile of your students and potential students. Start by asking the following questions:

1. What is the primary reason students typically come to your school?

2. What types of hobbies do your students typically have?

3. What current trends in culture will your students be interested in/want to know about?

4. What events locally and nationally are important to your students?

Let us look at these one by one.

1. What is the primary reason students typically come to your school.

Even without doing any marketing at all, your school will still attract students for certain reasons. What are those reasons?

Is it because of your athletic program? Do you have a sports team that is known nation-wide? If so, then keeping your audience updated with information about that team—interviews on ESPN, or coverage by Sports Illustrated—would be a really good idea.

What about academic programs? Is your school really well known for a particular discipline of study? If so, then share information about that profession or discipline as you find it from other sources. Again, you do not want to brag. Do not post about the program in your school ("all of our students get jobs"), but about the actual discipline ("Mechanical engineering is the ideal profession for this generation, according to this study").

Is it because it is close or convenient? In this case, the important factor may be value. Share information that others write regarding the school's value, costs and convenience.

In all likelihood it will be a combination of many things, which is good because it gives you a large amount of information to draw from and share. However, you must ensure that you are not spreading information potential students really do not care about.

2. What kinds of hobbies do your students have?

This could lead to a number of possible answers, which is good—the more the better, after all.

As I mentioned in the previous example, New Mexico Tech's students are, generally speaking, really into science fiction. So, administrators seek out and share information that somehow fits this interest. Maybe it is a piece of news about an upcoming film, or a classic TV show, like Dr. Who. The point is: it is an item that the audience will recognize and probably engage with.

However, schools like New Mexico Tech have a bit of an advantage over larger schools. In New Mexico Tech's case, the school is very niche-based, and so the students tend to, as a whole, resemble one another. In a larger, more varied student-body, it may not be as easy to identify interests to share content about. However, looking at it more generally could be a good idea.

So, for example, Instead of focusing on a particular genre of movie, simply focus on movies in general.

Or, if your intention is to attract the interest of a very niche-body of students, then focusing on those niche interests could be a very smart strategy.

3. What current trends in culture will your students be interested in/want to know about?

Being on top of trends is vitally important when campaigning through social media, because information travels so quickly and becomes outdated just as rapidly.

Drawing from what you know about your audience you can share information about current trends in popular culture that they will appreciate and be interested in.

The information you share does not make a difference, but somehow relating it to your school and students does.

Here is a quick example.

Rebecca Black entered notoriety with her YouTube video, *Friday*, back in early 2011. Before she knew it, she was an internet celebrity, known mostly for how bad her song/video/lyrics were. The infamy paid off in the form of hundreds of millions of views.

At the time the video came out and became viral most college and high school students—who after all spend more time on YouTube than any other demographic—were aware of it.

So, confident that the audience of their Facebook page would make the connection, administrators of New Mexico Tech's Facebook Page told fans of the page, "It is Friday, Friday, gotta get down on Friday"—a line from the song that sure enough people quickly recognized and responded to (with tongue-in-cheek groans of pain).

These types of posts create a fun and interesting atmosphere that students appreciate and are willing to engage with. They mirror the culture the student is a part of and indicate that your school is aware of what is going on in the world outside of the university.

4. What events locally and nationally are important to your students?

You can also give students information about what is going on locally, around the school, around the town or even around the state.

Concerts, art or cultural exhibits, sales or deals at restaurants: really the list of potential items is limitless.

Keeping your audience aware of these things demonstrates how dynamic your city or university is. Obviously, they want to be part of a school and community that offers distractions away from the books. By posting such items you give potential students the opportunity to see all that goes on at your school.

Likewise, students attending from away from home—not to mention the parents or those students—often worry about their new city and town. They want a vibrant place to live while at school. You can assume they will do some web-based research, but in all likelihood they may listen closely to what you have to say about it.

Aside from asking the four questions we just covered, there are some other obvious types of information you should try to share.

Information about your area: As mentioned before, students and their parents are often quite curious about the region or area that a university is in, so you can help them by sharing information about it.

Again, though, you do not want to brag or advertise: "Did you know this region has the best weather in the US?"

Instead, share information or reports that others have created to implicitly tell them why your region is so wonderful: "According to a new study, our city has the best weather in the US!"

The difference is subtle, but it is the difference between conversation and advertising.

Information about your school: This should be pretty obvious by now. You should share every piece of positive information that someone else says about you.

This could include news about your majors, your faculty, your marching band, your sports teams, your tuition and costs, your dorms: everything!

But again, it is information others have said about you. All you do is pass it along.

Importantly, though, these must be sprinkled throughout with the other kind of content that is not about you. If you posted nothing but information about you—even if someone else did say it—it would be put in the advertising column and then quickly ignored.

2. Where do you find this information?

The art of finding online content to pass along to others via social media is called "curating."

In a sense you are acting like the curator of a museum, or perhaps a reference librarian: pointing people to interesting and relevant information that they want to engage with.

Finding the information could be a full-time job, and quite frankly it is difficult if you do not have a starting place.

However, the questions in the previous section give you that starting place, and you use that information to track down new and relevant content to give to others.

Start by using the Google tool, Google Alerts. You can sign up for alerts to be delivered to your inbox on a daily basis about whatever topic you choose.

The most obvious place to begin is with your school's name—create alerts for as many variations as you can think of. Then create alerts for the town or region your school is in, the state and perhaps even part of the country (Southwest, Mid-South, etc.).

Next, sign up for RSS feeds from websites popular with your demographic—ESPN, Yahoo! News, etc.

Finally, create alerts or search for information that is very niche-oriented if you were able to identify some very niche topics.

Try to synch the alerts so they all arrive at the same time, at the beginning of the day so that you can draw from them to post throughout the rest of the day.

Some people like to post to their social media networks one time at the beginning of the week through an automated system that posts for them over the next seven days. While it is a good time-saver, your content will always be a week out of date and your audience is sure to have seen it already by the time you post it.

There are also other methods of spreading good or interesting information, and they depends on who you follow in the various networks (yes, you—your school that is—should follow others as well). We will look at how to do that when we cover each network by itself.

There are a couple of objectives you should have in mind when sharing this information. First, it should always be fresh (unless it is particularly relevant to something going on at the time). Otherwise it is a bore because your audience has probably already seen it.

Second, while you are trying to keep things interesting, you do not want to overwhelm the people who are getting your posts. Give them a chance to react and engage with you before posting something else.

Lastly, remember to mix it up. Un-marketing is the art of implicitly selling your brand. It is keeping your name in front of your audience on a consistent basis, drawing them to you, and getting them to become interested in you and what you have to say. This is not done through advertising, but at times you must spread information about yourself or they will never know anything about you. Make sure you mix enough entertainment/education/information about your school.

In chapters coming up we will closely examine specific social media channels and identify strategies you can use to find your ideal audience and get them to pay attention to you.

Action Items

1. Look at a brand that you feel has a very good presence on either Facebook or Twitter. What kind of information are they spreading?

2. Out of the last 10 posts or updates, how many talk about themselves?

3. Is there any user feedback to what they post? Do people share it or respond to it?

4. Create 10 Google Alerts that will help you find relevant information to share with your audience.

9 Create a Complete Facebook Presence for Admissions and Recruitment

This chapter will focus on the Facebook Pages that you as an admission and recruiting professional can create to drive enrollment and support your mission. You can also use this presence to create a more authentic relationship with potential students—connecting with them on a personal level and genuinely helping them.

A question I am often asked is, "How many Facebook pages are too many Facebook pages?"

Should each admission counselor/recruiter have his or her own, or should there merely be a single page for the admission office to support the school?

The answer depends on your school's unique circumstances. If you are part of a small or very focused school, then it would not make a lot of sense to have a number of pages each with only a few people following.

But if your school is large, with many people already trying to get in, then creating a page for each admission counselor might be a good idea, especially if those counselors often meet with students who are looking for specific advice about getting into the school, deadlines, financial aid etc.

The counselor could be the very personal contact that answers questions and ultimately helps the family make the decision about going to that particular school—and all via Facebook instead of face-to-face (the traditional method).

However, for the sake of this chapter, we will focus on a single page that represents the admission or recruiting office for your school. The strategies we use can be applied to just about any situation, though, so whatever you decide you will already be prepared.

1. Setting up Your Page

Let us start by simply creating a page. We are assuming you already have a Facebook profile/membership. If you do not, then simply go to http://www.facebook.com and sign up.

Difference between Pages and Profiles: Before we actually create the page, let us talk about why you need one in the first place. Many people do not understand the difference between a Facebook Page and a Personal Profile, and so they create a profile for their business instead of a professional page. This only creates problems in the future.

For starters, Facebook Pages are designed for professional organizations, and so they include features those organizations will need, including:

- Analytics features to track things like the number of interactions (likes, shares and comments) and user statistics (age, gender, geographic information, etc.).

- Marketing abilities like mass messaging so you can contact all of your followers at once.
- Advertising mechanisms so that you can buy ads on Facebook and send them to your page.
- The ability to create and use custom tabs, allowing you to include video or welcome pages, surveys, contact forms or feedback mechanisms.

Facebook profiles do not include any of these features. In addition, profiles require people to request to be your friend, whereas pages allow them to simply "Like" you to start viewing your posts.

Another important point is that Facebook profiles only allow you to have up to 5000 friends. Pages, on the other hand, allow you a limitless number of fans.

There are a ton of other differences you can read about on Facebook itself. The point is that Facebook has taken pains to really help businesses and organizations truly reach their fans.

So with that said, let us create your page.

1. After logging into Facebook, go to http://www.facebook.com/pages/create.php
2. Select Company, Organization or Institution.
3. Select University from the drop-down menu, and then fill in the name of your page.

   A word about names: I have seen some horrible Facebook names used for some very promising campaigns. Names alone will not make a campaign fail, but the right name you pick could make the difference between a prospective student remembering/finding/engaging with you, instead of another university.

4. Follow the steps for creating the page: including uploading and inserting a profile picture, cover picture, writing the info portion and including your contact information.

   Think carefully about the information you fill in here. This information helps people decide whether they want to interact with you, but it is also indexed on Google and other search engines, so the information you include here could be picked up in search results for your school name + admission.

5. Once you have filled in the information, invite people to Like the page.

   These should be your co-workers, others in the office, even friends and family. You essentially want to create a small group of fans so that potential fans (potential students, parents, etc.) will feel comfortable when deciding whether or not to also Like your page (nobody likes being the first person at the party, after all).

6. From here, set the page up as you would a house you were trying to sell: "stage it."

   Include pictures of your school, your admissions counselors, recruiting events, etc. Include videos if you have any that showcase your school, your majors and students.

   These social objects are necessary to help your potential students make the decision about your Facebook page (not your school). The more you have, the more potential there is for engagement.

7. The last step to take before adding your page to your recruitment strategy is to create your username for the page.
   a. Go to http://www.facebook.com/username
   b. Select the page from the drop down menu.
   c. Enter the username for this page.

The username is the name that follows www.facebook.com and should be short and memorable, like YourSchoolNameAdmissions.

Once you have selected the username, uploaded your images and videos, updated all of the proper information, you are ready to begin posting status updates.

2. Posting Status Updates—Content and Frequency

Facebook status updates are a crucial part of your strategy. They should be well thought out, planned, researched and created with a purpose.

What purpose?

Posts should be engineered to educate, inform and entertain your audience.

"About what," is probably what you are asking.

Think back to Chapter 7 and the general methods of un-marketing. Your posts should be about things that are interesting to your audience—from trends and popular culture, to news and current events. You can also post information about yourself and your school if it is something said by someone else (otherwise it is bragging and advertising).

You can share links to news articles, images and videos you find.

You can—and should—also create your own content through basic updates ("It is unbelievably cold today..."), or your own images and videos.

The frequency of these posts is another important factor. According to one study, you will reach about 20% of your followers by posting once every day, so that should be a minimum. Ideally, 2-3, well thought out and entertaining posts are what you need to carry out your strategy.

2-3 times a day you want to make your fans laugh, think, or otherwise respond to what you are posting.

3. Strategies for Finding Your Audience

The starting place for this phase is to understand who you want to connect with and what those people are like.

You have already done much of this: you know we are looking for the 14-17 year old demographic plus their influencers—parents to be exact.

Also by now you have taken the action steps in Chapter 7 and understand what your audience likes, is interested in, or pays attention to.

Now it is time to use that information to find your audience and attract them to you.

Getting Started

Before we start engaging people online through Facebook, I want to spend a moment talking about making them aware of you offline first.

You should make sure that a link to your Facebook page is at the footer of each of your website's pages, with a very explicit invitation to connect. Do the same for the footer of everyone's email as well.

Likewise, for every email you send on behalf of the school's recruiting effort, and even snail mail items like postcards, make sure an invitation to connect with you is prominent.

Finally, it should also go in every other piece of correspondence from your office or you: from viewbooks to business cards.

You do not want to miss any opportunity to connect with your audience through social media, because as we have discussed it allows you to stay engaged with them and provide them with information they need to decide on your school.

So, now we are ready to start actively pursuing our potential students. This is where the information about them becomes absolutely critical.

Put simply, you will go to the places they go, and engage with those places to get noticed by your audience.

Sound corny? Maybe so, but it works. And if you are being honest about your engagement (not making stuff up, for example, but being genuine) it is just like virtually visiting the students' high schools and talking to them there.

If for example the audience you want to engage with is particularly active on certain video game or movie fan pages, you—as your page—can comment and engage with that page and its visitors.

You can and should do the same for any of the other trends or likes you identify from your potential students or their parents.

To carry out these strategies you first—as your Facebook page—have to like *those* Facebook pages. To do this:

1. Go to your page
2. Select Admin Panel
3. Select Manage
4. Select Use Facebook as YourPageName
5. Navigate to the page you want to engage with and Like that page

Be sure to select the Use Facebook as YourPageName before leaving comments as well, otherwise they will show up with your personal name and profile instead of your page's name.

Another place you can use this strategy is on the blogs that your students might read. By selecting the Use Facebook as YourPageName button, you can surf the internet and interact with blogs as your Facebook page through certain commenting platforms, like Disqus (www.disqus.com), which links your Facebook profile to the blog comments (in this case the Facebook profile the comment would be attributed to would be the page you created).

At first, as long as you are logged into Facebook, you will see your own profile image next to the comment box, but if you simply select "Change" next to the "Comment as Your Name" text, you can select and comment as your page.

If you do not like the idea of reaching out to students through their likes, interests or hobbies, then engage with the areas they or their parents will be going to as part of their college search: SAT/ACT prep sites, articles and Facebook pages, college admission sites and articles, career sites and articles, etc.

You should go to these sites at the very minimum, because they offer the potential for attracting not only your future students, but their parents as well. And as we have already discussed, social media users are extremely susceptible to the opinions of their friends and family (their influencers).

Another method of attracting followers is through a targeted Facebook ad campaign. This can be very effective when carried out correctly. There are many stages to this type of campaign, like understanding what narrow demographic you want to attract. I say "narrow" because you cannot possibly target every high school student in the country, or even your state.

Instead, try focusing on specific students who themselves are looking for something very specific. If you have a particularly good forensic anthropology degree you could target high school students in a particular area who are fans of CSI.

Of course you would want to send them to a location that highlights your CSI degree, so you would have to prepare a custom landing tab (Google this phrase if you are unfamiliar with it).

Before starting a project like this, think carefully about your goals and objectives. Do you want to attract followers or create awareness for something, like a degree or scholarship? These are two explicitly different purposes, after all. It is doubtful that you might gain followers with the above strategy at first, but given time you may pick up those who become more and more interested in your school and that particular program.

4. Creating Engagement

Once you have followers you want to keep them, and more importantly you want to create engagement.

Studies have found that the majority of people who like your page will simply watch and listen, so you want to keep them watching and listening to you. That is why sharing interesting, educating and relevant information is so important.

You also want to give opportunities for engagement for those who will decide post comments or engage in other ways.

This is accomplished through same methods as simply entertaining them and keeping them interested in the first place.

However, there are more explicit methods of creating engagement. One tried and true strategy is simply to ask them questions. The questions could be about a variety of things, and should run the gambit from the serious ("Did anyone watch the presidential debate last night?") to the more humorous ("What would you use to kill zombies if they attacked?").

The point is to get reactions—positive reactions—to what you say, post, think and do. Talk about current events, about trendy items, and about items from popular culture. Also talk about what college is like, how they can find financing, where to look for jobs, what types of majors are getting hired after graduation, and where to live.

Then, on occasion, talk about yourself.

What you will soon find is that out of perhaps 1000 followers, you will see comments and interaction from the same 20 or so. These are the people who will most likely share your content and refer others to you, do not be afraid of addressing them personally.

Ultimately, the goal of social media is to be social. So do that. Get to know your potential students, answer their questions and take the time to discuss their concerns about one of the biggest steps in their lives.

If some of them do not end up going to your school, then at least you know that you have honestly tried to help them in their future.

5. General Tips and Strategies

In closing I would like to leave you with some last pieces of advice I have learned over the last several years.

For starters, do not forget that the internet—regardless of what platform (your website or Facebook page)—is a visual medium. Facebook is especially good at organizing and sharing content and media. Take advantage of this as much as possible.

From taking pictures of squirrels on your campus to videos of a parade through the town your college is in, everything you share has the potential of reaching the one person who is just destined to go to school there.

Second, understand the limitations of Facebook. Every now and then even social media marketing experts forget the rule about advertising through social media. Try your best to remember that you are building relationships that will pay off over time, not immediately.

Lastly, approach Facebook honestly. Look at it as a platform for helping people find answers to questions. Be there to really help them, not just to try to recruit them. Yes, recruiting is our final goal, but that is not going to happen if the people you interact with sense that all you want is to get them in the door.

Be an advisor and advocate to your Facebook fans. Really try to educate, inform and entertain them with the information you provide. If you take this approach your Facebook campaign will be successful.

Action Items

1. Search Facebook for the recruiting or admissions page to another university.

2. What are they posting and how frequently?

3. How often are people engaging them and what are they saying?

4. How many fans do they have and who are they?

10 Tweeting your School

Once again I am going to assume your school has a Twitter account, a number of followers, and is tweeting regularly (none of which means it is doing it correctly, by the way).

Here we are going to focus on a Twitter account for you as an admission's official. If you would like you can exchange yourself and your own account for a single account for your office, but as we will see in a moment, Twitter is quite different than Facebook, which may make you want to create your own space.

1. Basics

Twitter is perhaps the most misunderstood of the many social networks. It has well over 100 million users and is very popular among the young and educated, but many do not understand how to use it professionally (which is what we will cover here).

As a platform, it is much more dynamic and fast-moving than Facebook. It is also much more public. Connecting with people is also easier, as is creating an identity.

2. Creating your Profile

We will start creating your profile by first signing up for an account on www.twitter.com.

Continue through the registration process as you personally and not your office.

We want to do this because for the time being, the features of every account are identical—unlike Facebook in which a personal profile had limited features when compared to business or professional pages.

Also, because college recruiting is so personal, creating a presence as a person (as opposed to an office in the school) is much more preferable. Parents and students want to feel safe and secure in talking to someone they might then see if they visit your school, or maybe talk to on the phone if they have a problem.

In the registration process there are a couple of areas I would like you to really think about.

The first is your bio.

Your bio is a vitally important piece of your Twitter presence. The words you use act like keywords and are used to help find you when users enter those keywords. They are also used by Twitter to suggest you to other users, who may then follow you because of what they see in your profile.

Certain words stand out and you will see that when you create your profile you may immediately get followers.

People often ask, "How did they find me so quickly?"

The answer is the bio and the words you used. If you used the key words "real estate" in your bio, you might suddenly find yourself followed by people in the real estate industry.

Many people have searches saved, and they will quickly be pointed to you simply because the keywords in your bio match the keywords they have set up their automatic search to find (we will cover these for you in a bit).

Space is limited to only 160 characters so definitely think about brevity. However, do not just write a series of keywords separated by commas, instead make it meaningful. For example:

"Admission official with State University, helping students enroll in college, find financial assistance, transition from high school, and create a bright future"

That is exactly 160 characters and contains some valuable keywords, including the name of the school. Your bio can be changed, so do not stress about it too much right now. Create one that makes sense and reads well, and come back to it for tweaking as needed.

3. Image and Page Design

The image you use is important too, because it shows up next to every single one of your tweets. Use a professional portrait if you can, otherwise a nice image of you in action "professionally"—talking to students or speaking at a conference—would be a great idea and would reinforce the identity you are creating.

Your image also shows up prominently in search results immediately next to your name. Studies have found that people quickly make a decision about following someone because of the image they use. Silly and shallow, perhaps, but the goal is to get followed (and by the right people), so it is still an important point.

You can customize the design of your page, and probably should, to connect who you are with what you do. You can upload background images, such as images of your school, sports team, etc. You can also select the colors and page design you want to use.

There are also literally hundreds of companies on the web that provide custom backgrounds for Twitter. Some are free—usually with the company's web address place prominently somewhere—while other cost a small fee.

Try to connect each of the elements in your profile—image, background colors, and font color and style—with the school you are representing.

You are doing this for a number of reasons. The most obvious is to create brand awareness for your school. A less obvious reason is to create an element of trust that you want your followers to have in you. You are an authority figure, after all, and an expert in both your school and school admissions. As such you want to portray this through the design of your page.

Now that you are set up let us talk about how to tweet.

4. Tweeting—content and frequency

The content you tweet is the same kind of content you would post on Facebook: items that educate, inform, entertain and which are relevant.

They are, of course, much more brief—limited to 140 total characters—and are often meant to send followers somewhere else (to external links, images or videos).

Find content similar to the content you would post for Facebook—news articles, funny videos, interesting images, etc. However, separate the content from Facebook (in other words, tweet different content than your status updates might contain).

You also want to tweet much more frequently than you post on Facebook, perhaps as much as every half hour. I know that sounds impossible, but you only have a split second to gain someone's attention until you build a presence that they begin to closely watch.

Charlie Sheen can post once every couple of days and be confident that many will read what he says the occasion that he says it because people are actually looking for his tweets. Until you reach that point, you need to tweet as much as you can.

There are tools and websites that we will look at later to make Twitter posting much, much easier, so do not fret about where you will find the time to post as much as you need to.

5. Strategies for Finding Your Audience and Gaining Followers

Gaining followers on Twitter is actually pretty simple, but what we want to focus on is getting quality follows, not just any follow.

The first method is to start following others.

Twitter is less personal than Facebook, and so people often follow others generally because they are interested in what they have to say, their bio sounds intriguing, or their tweets are entertaining. For one reason or another, people follow lots of other people on Twitter.

So, the best place to start is something akin to the strategy suggested for Facebook. Find Twitter users your audience will follow, and then follow them. I do not necessarily mean celebrities or pop icons (unless you are really interested enough to follow them), I mean college prep organizations, ACT/SAT prep businesses, News channels, newspaper, and anyone else you can think of.

On Twitter there is typically a sense of payback, and you will quickly notice that as you follow someone they in turn follow you back.

You will also notice that people following the people you follow, will also then follow you, and the cycle repeats.

Another method of getting followers is simply by putting out good content. When someone shares your tweet with their followers it is called a retweet (or RT for short). Retweets can be powerful mechanisms for gaining new followers.

As you send out a tweet that for one reason or another is shareable (it is funny, it is relevant, it contains valuable information, etc.), your followers may retweet you, which then places your content in front of *their* followers.

You will find you gain a huge number of followers this way.

Still another method, and perhaps one of the most important considering our final goal, is to use Twitter search (search.twitter.com).

Twitter search lets you see what is being said about a particular topic in real time, and saved searches notify you when someone has tweeted using the keyword or phrase you entered.

Imagine how valuable this can be.

When a student enters a phrase like "picking a college" you are alerted about it immediately.

The next step is to respond. In this case you want to be as "hands-off" as possible so you do not look creepy or like a stalker. However, this is part of what you want to do—offer an invitation to engage.

Let us extend our example so you can see what I mean.

Twitter user @jack1992, a high school student, tweets, "I'm having a tough time deciding what college I want to go to."

Because you have "college" as a saved search you receive a notification.

You send a tweet that says, "@jack1992 I understand what you are going through. I am an admission counselor at State University, let me know if you need any advice or help"

94

The user may or may not respond, but at the very least you have reached out a hand. You are not pushy, and you are not even advertising your school, you are only offering to help.

And remember, that is the point: helping students, not just getting them to enroll.

This is social media marketing in a nutshell. This method will gain you followers and, more importantly, will put you in front of the exact people you want to be in front of.

6. Creating Engagement

Engagement through Twitter is much more personal than through Facebook. When someone comments on a Facebook post, everyone who sees the post can also see the comment.

Likewise, when *you* make a comment, it is also seen by your followers.

And these posts stick around for awhile—they could remain on someone's stream for hours depending on their settings.

Tweets are much more fast-moving when compared to Facebook posts, which is why you have to create them with much more frequency.

However, interacting and engaging with tweets is also much more dynamic and ephemeral—they simply do not stay around very long for others to see.

But, *you* see these interactions. When someone uses your Twitter name (called a "handle") on Twitter, it displays in your "interactions" and "mentions" tabs (and it is actually called, "being mentioned").

This occurs when people reply directly to a tweet you sent—they agree with you, disagree with you, or simply want to tell you how they feel about what you said.

As in the case of Facebook, it is important to reply to these interactions because it shows that you are actually listening and, more importantly, that you actually care. It may get tiresome at times to reply to every mention you get, but it will increase the loyalty of the follower you are engaging.

When people retweet what you say they are essentially broadcasting you to their followers, which is one of the points of crafting well thought out tweets.

It is common practice on Twitter to mention those people who retweet you and thank them after they do so. Doing this builds good will and encourages them and others to retweet you just to get the mention.

As with Facebook you can also initiate interaction by retweeting, replying to, or otherwise engaging the content that others send out. Sometimes it is smart to make quick replies personally to someone's tweet just to maintain the interpersonal relationships you build through Twitter. This interaction is appreciated and always welcomed.

Hashtags are also frequently used to garner engagement. In Twitter, when a 'pound symbol,' or 'hash tag,' (#) is placed before a word, the word becomes linked to every other instance of that word (or group of joined words).

If you click on a hashtag in a tweet, you will then see all other tweets that might use that same hashtag.

So, for example, the phrase, #PresidentialElection, is a hashtag because it begins with the pound symbol. Any tweets containing this hashtag get aggregated together into a single stream.

For the purposes of engagement, know that many people have searches saved for these hashtags, especially for hashtags containing new or trendy subject matter (think of the name of current events, like #SuperBowl, etc.).

Including hashtags in your tweets—especially relevant or trendy hashtags—will undoubtedly get you found by other people conducting searches. Then, they may choose to follow or engage you.

Still another method of reaching your audience is through direct messaging (DM's as they are called). Experts frown on using this mechanism, especially in using it extensively to contact your followers, because it is often associated with "spam" and you are sure to get "unfollowed" very quickly.

In closing, Twitter is a time-consuming mechanism that requires creativity and strategy to be used correctly. Many get frustrated very early when using Twitter and never see it reach its full potential.

However, if you can make it through the first few months of using and learning to use it, the payoff could be quite large. Twitter allows you to build a national brand, not just a local or regional. You will find that you can target even more precisely than you can in Facebook, that followers are very loyal and interactive, and that they often follow your advice, guidance and opinions.

As we will see, Twitter should be a crucial piece of your overall strategy, and as the platform grows it promises to become and even more important piece in the years to come.

Action Items

1. Search Twitter for admission counselors from other schools. What do their bios look like?

2. Do a search for "picking a college" and see if you come up with any results. If you do, what would be the next step you would take?

3. Create your bio. Now do a search for the keywords in your bio and see what you come up with.

11 Videos and YouTube

Videos are probably one of the best ways to spread content online. They are cheap to make, easy to share, convenient to watch, and popular amongst your primary demographic. They are also one of the best ways for you to showcase your school, students, campus, activities—virtually everything that makes you, you.

Likewise, potential students and influencers appreciate organizations— any organizations—that give behind-the-scene looks, regardless of how brief or how high or low the production value is.

Videos increase your ranking on search engine results and provide an outlet for engagement and interaction.

There is a good chance your school has a YouTube channel already, in which case the best option is to utilize that channel for the videos you upload expressly for recruitment. If this is the case, ask the administrator of the channel to create a Playlist just for you.

Playlists are methods of categorizing videos in a channel. Your school might already have a playlist for lectures, for example, or even for specific lecture topics (physics, chemistry, etc.). Creating one, or a few of your own, allows you to control the content specifically for that playlist.

However, if your school does not yet have a channel—or you want to set up a channel for your office—we will briefly go through the process of setting one up.

1. Creating and Modifying a YouTube Channel

Creating a YouTube Channel is fairly easy and self-explanatory: simply go to http://www.youtube.com and select, "Create Account"

You will then have to create a new Google account.

If you already have an account with Google you are free to use that. However, if you are creating a channel for either your school or your office—admissions or recruiting—then it would be a better idea to create a brand new Google and then YouTube account (after all, other people will be using this password and username combination).

Once you have selected the link that is sent to the email address you can sign in, using the username and password you created.

A word about user names: Your YouTube Channel will be associated with the username you choose and will read, www.YouTube.com/UserName.

If you are going to create a channel for your school, then you should be consistent with other brands on social media platforms. So, if on Facebook the school's username is Facebook.com/StateUniversity, choose the same for YouTube (and all other social media platforms).

If the channel is for the admission or recruiting office, choose a name that makes sense, like StateUniversityRecruiting.

2. Channel Design and Organization

As with Twitter you should create a custom design for your channel, and it should be consistent with the look of your other social media platforms—or your web presence. Choose the colors that your school uses, upload the school's logo as a background and profile image, and generally try to clearly brand your channel to reflect your school.

Be sure to completely fill out your profile so that you are easily found if someone is searching the topics of higher education recruiting, or even your school. Include as many details in your profile as possible.

If you are creating the channel for your school, you can add it to the YouTube's EDU section (http://www.youtube.com/education).

Only colleges and universities are allowed in this section, and being admitted carries some perks. For example, you have the ability to immediately upload videos of any length (basic YouTube accounts are at first limited to 15 minutes or less than 3GB).

3. Creating and Uploading Videos

We are going to focus on the types of videos you should be creating to help your effort. In summary, you should create videos about absolutely everything you possibly can!

Remember that videos typically rank higher than websites on search engine results, so the more you have about topics your target audience is searching for, the more likely you will rank towards the top. And, getting to the top of search engine results is typically the difference between 10 people watching a video and 1000.

Think about all of the things that potential students, their parents, and high school counselors want to know about your school before they make a choice about going there (or recommending someone else go there).

Where will they live? What do the dorms look like? What is in the meal plan? What scholarships can they get? Where do they find this information? What is there to do on campus? What is there to do off-campus? How safe is campus or the town?

The list is endless.

I know what you are thinking: all of that stuff is already on your website. Well, it may be there in text, it may have nice pictures on it, and it may even get a lot of views, but videos will increase—maybe even double—the amount of exposure this information gets. Plus, as I said, it could rank you above competition.

Plus—and this is a very important 'plus' in terms of social media—the webpages on your site are static. They do not allow people to comment or ask questions right there in the website. YouTube videos, as we have covered earlier, allow people to provide feedback through the comments section. YouTube also allows users to share those videos with other people via different social media platforms.

It takes time to do this, but not as much as you might think. In as little as one hour per day you can create 2-3 videos and cover all of the topics above and more.

Some other videos you might want to consider making—and some that your audience might even expect—are 'interview' videos.

Potential students—and their parents—are often very curious about the students who go to your school. This is the natural product of questions they ask themselves: "will I fit in there," "will I be able to make friends there," etc.

You should try to make a number of these videos by interviewing students from different walks of life and in different majors.

Also, try to take some videos of lectures, especially of popular professors or classes. These should be the full extent of the lectures and not simply the introductions or brief portions of them. YouTube seems to value these lectures more than other videos, and even classifies them in a special category specific to college lectures.

The quality of these videos does not have to be, nor are they expected to be, as high as you might think.

Your demographic has grown up in an age of instant digital information, and information shared by other users. They are used to seeing videos made on cell phone cams, web cams, and other, low-quality video cameras.

This does not mean that you should try to make low-quality videos. Instead you should try to make videos with high-quality content. Your audience will forgive the quality once you answer their questions.

So focus on the content of these videos first.

Have your graphic designers give you a logo to insert at the beginning of the video to brand it with your school and also include the name and contact details of your office.

You can include annotations in the video through YouTube itself, so you do not need a very robust video editing system. Microsoft Movie Maker or Adobe Premiere Elements are two software programs that will give you all of the tools you will need to edit and splice video. They are both inexpensive and easy to use as well.

The camera you use is also less important than the content of the videos. However there are some considerations to make.

You want something small and portable so you can easily carry it with you at events or just around campus. It should be easy to operate and not overly complicated. Remember, we are trying to simply make as many videos as we can to answer questions, improve search engine rankings, and share information.

One consideration to keep in mind is the audio quality. If you decide to film interviews with students you will want to use some type of lavalier or wireless microphone so interviewees can easily be heard.

Lighting might be something to also think about, especially if many of the situations you plan on filming will be low-light conditions.

4. Getting Content Views

Once you have created a video—or many videos—you want to ensure people will actually find them and view them. The first step, obviously, is to get them uploaded to YouTube.

When you do there are some details to keep in mind.

First, you should create a short but very informative title that is filled with keywords your audience will look for.

Something like "A Dorm Room at State University" might certainly explain what the video is about, but "What Do the Dorm Rooms Look Like at State University" will probably be what the student is actually searching for, so calling it that will ensure it is more easily found.

Another consideration is deciding what to include in the video's description. This can be as long as you would like it to be, but should also be filled with the keywords your audience may be searching for.

You may also want to include the latitude and longitude (or the address) of where the video was taken. If this information is filled in, whenever someone does a Google search for that particular location, the video will be included with the results, and so may be viewed. Likewise, if someone enters that location or is at the location using mobile platforms like Google Maps, there is a chance the video might be displayed as location information.

Another step you can take to ensure views is to share the video in as many places as you can. You can post a link to the video on college entrance forums, on your Facebook page, on Twitter, etc.

Every time you share the video through a link or other method, you increase the chances that your target audience will see it and engage with it.

5. Creating Engagement

Engagement—in regards to YouTube—means a couple of different things. It could mean comments and responses to your videos. It could simply mean feedback in the form of likes or dislikes. It also means attracting channel subscribers.

All of these methods bring you closer to your target audience, and all should be objectives—though they should not be as important as your primary objective: getting video views.

YouTube viewers often do not comment on videos as much as users of other platforms. But when people do comment or ask a question, always take the time to answer them. Thank them if they have left positive feedback or negative. If they do ask a question, be sure to answer it completely and even invite them to email or call you.

Having a base of subscribers to your channel is also important. The more subscribers you have the more likely it is that others will watch and share your videos.

You can get more subscribers much in the same way you get followers and fans on other platforms—you subscribe to other channels. This puts your name in front of people who may be looking at those channels.

You can also leave comments on videos that your target audience may watch. Use your common sense here, obviously you only want to subscribe to and comment on channels and videos that are in good taste and relevant.

Understand the objectives for creating a social media-based video campaign. While on other platforms you want to engage with students to help them in their transition to college, here you want to simply give them information in a forum and format they are very likely to see.

Your goals then should be video views and top-of-mind awareness for your school, and not necessarily high levels of engagement.

Action Items

1. Write down every question you have been asked about your school in the past year by either students or their parents.
2. Rank those questions according to which are asked more frequently and often.
3. Use this list to create your videos, and prioritize from the most often asked to the least.

12 Blogging for Students

Five years ago, if you said you had a blog people probably thought you wore tight fitting pants, had a hipster haircut and lived with your parents. You probably wrote about your life, your perceptions about art or music, and you generally treated the blog as your personal journal (as in when we used to write on paper type of journal), only you allowed anyone in the world to read it.

And in truth, much of that might have been accurate. In many ways, though, blogs have changed (though, sadly, the negative perception has not). For a school looking to reach potential students and their influencers, a blog could be the most powerful tool in your digital marketing arsenal.

If you are not familiar with blogs (short for weblogs), they are brief articles that relay a small amount of content about a particular subject, which are published on a personal or business website, or special blog website.

And, as we saw in Chapter 3 they are very popular. Let me repeat a statistic we looked at earlier: according to one producer of a popular blogging platform—WordPress—its software is used on over 66 million sites around the world. If that is not astounding, consider this: WordPress is only one of dozens of platforms.

For universities, what is even more important is the amount of reach these blogs and their articles get. In the same article that mentioned the previous statistic, WordPress also reported that the blogs powered by its platform are read by over 321 million visitors every month.

Blogs let schools and admission counselors reach potential students in a completely new and relevant way. They are mechanisms to teach them about a degree, a department, a professor, or even a campus, and they can show students and parents a different side of the school than they might normally see.

And if done right blogs may also increase the likelihood of being placed near the top of search results—the Holy Grail of online marketing.

If you are not sure about blogging, feel a bit queasy about it or are worried that you or your school will appear juvenile or unprofessional, be comforted in knowing that some of the largest companies on the planet—like IBM, Intel, Boeing, and Dell—have blogging campaigns.

1. Where to Start

There is a good chance you will have to talk to your website administrators to create a blog platform to use, and you will probably be at their mercy when it comes to which platform and how usable it is. However there are a few things you can request that will make your blog really useful to your overall campaign.

First, ask for an easy method for users to share the blog article. The reason that blogs are considered social media, and not just normal media, is they allow readers to interact and engage, and sharing is one of the measurements of that engagement.

The more your blog article is shared, the more popular the article is, the more readers you are reaching, and (hopefully) the more potential students you are helping and drawing in to you.

Most blog articles have methods for easily sharing the article via the most popular forms of social media and social networks, including Twitter, Facebook and LinkedIn.

It is also helpful to give readers the ability to share your article via social bookmarking sites.

We talked only briefly about social bookmarking sites because they are fairly specific to blogs and web-based articles. However, social bookmarking sites, like StumbleUpon, Digg, Reddit and Tumblr, allow people to save your article in categories they define for later reading.

What makes these sites "social" is that they allow people to also share your articles with others by tagging them with specific keywords and placing them in categories. Most members of these sites subscribe to a few or to many categories, and so if your article is tagged and placed in one of them other readers could possibly see it and it is potentially shared with them.

Organizations, such as your school, can also become members of these sites and then can scour the web to collect articles, including your own, that others could read.

Members can also become friends with other members, and then can see whatever their friends are subscribing to or reading.

Most blogging platforms allow readers to simply select one of a set of icons on the page to quickly and conveniently share the blog article—in the form of a link, title and perhaps description—with their networks.

Including these icons and this method for sharing is essential for blogging, and should be one of the primary mechanisms you request.

Another mechanism you need is a tool for readers to leave comments about your article. Remember that what separates social media from traditional media is the ability to provide feedback and interact with both the authors (you) and the content (your article).

Ask your web administrator or developer to create a method that allows people to leave comments in some format that can also be shared to social media. One platform, Disqus (www.disqus.com) allows users to leave comments via either their Twitter or Facebook profile. They can also share this comment, or at least make known the fact they left a comment, on either of these two networks (remember, the more your content is shared, or that people know about it, the more likely it will be seen and read).

2. What to Blog

Surprisingly the topic that makes people most anxious is not how to set up their blog or which platform to use, but what they should actually blog about.

This is a legitimate worry. After all, blogs do stem from people talking about their feelings, their Care Bear collection, or their mom's cooking.

But what do professionals write about?

The simple answer runs in tandem to what you should be making videos about: everything.

Like your videos, blog articles should be designed for three purposes: to attract people to read them through the strategic use of keywords, to provide useful and helpful information to potential students and their parents (or other influencers), and to create engagement. These three cover a lot of potential material.

Attract Readers through the Strategic Use of Keywords

Keywords are elements of text people enter into search engines in common search queries. Often they are combinations of words that make up "key phrases" or strings of key words.

The frequency of keywords on a website's pages is an element that helps search engines rank that page in terms of importance and placement in query results.

And this is an oh-so-important factor when trying to attract readers for your article or even visitors to your website.

According to a 2011 study, the top three results of a search query on Google accounted for 58.4% of all clicks (18). Any site that falls below the top three is competing for just over 40% of the traffic. You can imagine the consequences if your article is on the second or third page: virtually no visitors at all.

So you need to make sure to put the important phrases and words that your target audience is searching for prominently at the beginning of the article, and if possible even in the title.

How do you know what words or phrases are actually being searched for? You can use tools like Google Adwords Keyword Analyzer to understand how best to use a phrase. This tool will help you understand, for example, whether you should use "dorm rooms" or simply "dorms."

Also think about the questions students and parents often ask you. What are the top 10 questions you usually get? Using the question as the title, and then repeating it again in the first sentence, will force you to use keywords and phrases most likely used by your audience. Start with the first 10 you can think of, and then continue adding more to the list.

Provide Useful and Helpful Information to Potential Students and their Parents

Perhaps this is most important. To be authentic and taken seriously, your blog should be filled with useful information that students and their parents (i.e., your audience) want to find and read.

As in the previous section, think about the questions they will have. What are the dorms like? What is there to do on and off campus? What is the best degree to get? Who are the professors to take?

Also, think about things they will need to know, whether they go to your school or not. When do they need to apply for financial aid? When do they need to decide on a major? What are the requirements for scholarships?

Providing information like this will not only help your audience by providing them with useful and necessary information, but it will also help you as well. You do not want to be seen as someone who simply wants get students through the door. Instead, you want to be seen as someone who actually cares about the potential students, whether they go to your school or not.

By providing information that is in no way advertising or gratuitously promoting your school, you stand a better chance of becoming a trustworthy advisor to your readers, which will actually bring them closer to you and increase the likelihood they attend your school—or at least investigate it.

Create Engagement

As is the case for all other platforms, we want to create as much engagement as we can in our blog articles.

We mentioned previously that engagement in the sense of blogs means sharing the article and/or commenting on it.

112

The most obvious way to start is—as previously suggested—to make sure you have included the mechanisms for doing this. Without them you really do not have a blog article, you have a webpage: static and boring that really does no work for you.

Another method, which is just so common-sensical it pains me to mention it, is to ask for the engagement. So few blog writers do this.

At the end of the article, simply ask the reader what he or she thinks. Ask if the readers have any questions about the article, and state that if they do they can leave a comment that you will answer. Also, ask the reader to share the article if they liked it or to pass it along to someone who might find the information useful. You would be surprised how much this simple method actually helps.

Yet another method is to share the article yourself in as many places as you can. We have already mentioned social bookmarking sites, but you should also share all of your articles on your Facebook and Twitter profiles. You will find that your followers might not comment directly in the article comment section, but instead through these platforms, which—if your goal is simply to create engagement—should be just fine.

3. Get your Blog Read

The final question to consider is how to get your blog read by your target audience. This is perhaps the most crucial element. After all if nobody reads it, then what is the point?

Despite all of the effort we go through to ensure the article uses keywords and phrases, there is still much more that can and should be done to garner readers for your article.

The first is to spread it around yourself. As I have suggested for other reasons, you should share your blog article on your Facebook page and your Twitter stream.

There are mechanisms that will help you do this automaticlly, such as RSS reader applications to automatically get each new article you write as it is published. The reader then submits them to Facebook and/or Twitter at time-increments you specify.

You should also create an account for your school on the various social bookmarking sites, and then submit your articles to them.

Another method is to refer to your articles in the comment sections of blogs and articles at other sites. Look for articles from news agencies or organizations related to higher education, and then comment in one of those articles. In your comment, include the link back to your blog article.

As I mentioned earlier, one of the ways to ensure your article is ranked higher on search engine results is to include relevant keywords. Another method that search engines use is to measure the number of links that point to your article: the more links that trace back to your blog and to specific articles, the better.

You can also create an email list of people to send your article to. Somewhere on your site, have your web administrator create a form that simply submits someone's name and email address (the less information the more likely you will get them to give you their email address).

On Facebook, Twitter and elsewhere (like your site), advertise the fact that you email your articles out on a regular basis. You will be surprised how many people sign up.

You can also offer an RSS feed and tell people to subscribe to that as well. RSS—or Real Simple Syndication—is a method of syndicating your new articles. By subscribing to an RSS feed, a feed reader—a software on a user's computer or internet-based account like Google—will gather anything new that is written and released from a website, and deliver it to a user.

Also, simply put, the more you write, the more you will be read. Search engines index according to frequency, and so as you write more and as you write often, Google and other engines find your new content and place it in search engine results.

Ultimately, it comes down to time. It takes time for your articles to get indexed by search engines, and so it will take time for people to find them. Luckily, because colleges and universities often have high-valued content that is updated frequently, they are indexed very often. Once you begin, your articles are sure to start showing up in search query results within 30-45 days.

Action Items

1. Using Google or some other search engine, search one of the most frequently asked questions from parents or potential students.

2. Go through the search results and see if you find any blog articles. If so, what organizations were they published by? Are there any universities in the results?

3. Are there any questions you cannot find any results for (or can only find a few results for)? Make a list of these, and begin your blog writing with these as articles.

13 Tools to Make Your Life Easier

One of the most daunting things about sustaining a social media marketing campaign—which can last a long time after all—is trying to figure out when you have the time to actually make the status updates, tweets and posts that you need to make in order to keep your audience engaged. My recommendations are that Facebook updates should occur 2-3 times every day and Twitter updates about every hour or half hour. In the case of blogs I suggest at least once a week if not more.

But then there is the reality. Admission counselors are away all the time. They are on the road, visiting high schools, going to college fairs or conferences. What little time they spend in the office is devoted to looking at applicants' files, completing paperwork and planning, and arranging schedules for the next trip.

So how do you manage?

Well, luckily this is not only a problem for admission counselors and college recruiters. Business owners and others who rely on social media campaigns have had the same problems for years. Unless you are in the position to carry out the campaign full-time the problem will actually always exist.

Very early on many software companies took notice of this problem and set about creating programs to help. Five of the most popular in use today are:

1. Hootsuite (www.hootsuite.com)

2. Media Funnel (www.mediafunnel.com)

3. Seesmic (www.seesmic.com)

4. Tweetdeck (www.tweetdeck.com)

5. Social Oomph (www.socialoomph.com)

All five of these platforms carry out essentially the same functions, and all have free and premium (paid-for) services. Also, each platform has a free app that you can download to your smart phone or mobile device to update from the road or when you are otherwise out of the office.

To be clear, there are as of yet no good tools to help with YouTube, but because updates and posts are less frequent this should not pose as much of a problem.

Here we will review some of the features of these platforms and discuss how they could be especially useful for you as you plan and carry out the social media marketing strategies in this book.

1. Scheduled updates

One of my personal favorite features: these platforms allow you to create Twitter or Facebook updates ahead of time, and then schedule the exact time and date you want them to post. The scheduling can be well in advance so you can get holiday greetings out of the way all at once if you like.

You can imagine how helpful this is when you are faced with travelling or otherwise being out of the office or away from a desk.

In addition to scheduling updates, these platforms allow you to include social objects—videos, images or links—in the scheduled updates. They further will allow you to do all of this via mobile devices and smart phones. You can email posts and social objects to your accounts or use them (via their apps) directly from your phone.

2. View multiple channels at once

When trying to manage multiple channels it is often difficult to switch between them to see what is being said or where it is being said. This is especially true if you are managing multiple profiles in the same platform (multiple Twitter or Facebook profiles) because they typically only allow one profile open in a browser at a time.

These platforms can also allow you to set the view that you prefer, so that you can quickly see mentions, replies, retweets or comments. You also have the option of seeing your followers' streams or status, and for creating, saving and viewing the results of searches.

3. Manage team updating

If you have multiple people managing your Facebook or Twitter presences you will want to ensure that there is some administrative oversight. This is especially true if work-study or student employees will be making changes and updates.

Each platform has group management abilities, so that you can assign various users to different channels. Perhaps as important is the capability of assigning them roles in their work as well. So while giving someone the ability to write status updates or tweets for a certain channel, you can choose to not give them the ability to publish that update. Instead, the post gets held and awaits approval from a moderator before it is published.

You can see the obvious upside to this option: tweets and status updates get vetted before they become public. There is a downside to doing this however that you may also want to consider. One of the purposes of social media as a marketing device is that it is very quick to use. Creating a "permission-flow" (to coin a phrase), brings down the speed and ease with which social media is used.

4. Provide analytics

Each platform has its own analytics mechanism. As we will see in the chapter on Measuring your Return on Investment, understanding the analytics of your effort is extremely important.

What makes the analytics mechanisms on these platforms even more helpful is that they typically provide much more than the native social media platforms (Facebook and Twitter) do.

While each will tell you how many fans or followers you have—only Facebook will give you a full breakdown of your followers (demographics at least). The management platforms we are discussing here will help you get this kind of information for Twitter, as well as trends in the number of followers (when you are getting them, and how often) and an analysis of interactions for each.

Some of the platforms also provide reporting mechanisms (something which neither Facebook nor Twitter do as of yet), making it very simple to create status reports for your administration or your team.

5. Support for blogging

While most platforms focus on Facebook and Twitter, some (like Social Oomph) also have blogging capabilities as well. In fact, many blogging platforms provide helpful tools so that you can manage blogging on a regular schedule.

WordPress, for example, allows you to publish now or at a set time in the future. This is helpful once again if you are only in the office for a brief period—you could write 2-3 blog posts and schedule their publication over the next 2-3 weeks.

Conclusion

Social media campaigns require a lot of diligence, simply because people really need to see your name in front of them often to even remember you. Getting followers and fans to engage requires a constant effort: some will respond to one post while others will respond to another (and some will respond to nothing). So posting often is one key to success in social media campaigns (as is posting different kinds of information).

Social media management tools, like those mentioned, will help you create a sustained and successful social media campaign for your school.

Action Items

1. Write down everything you think you may need from a social media management platform.

2. What are the most important capabilities it should have?

3. Go look at the platforms provided at the beginning of this chapter and see which one best meets the capabilities you need.

Wandlys... for example allow you to publish a tweet at a certain time in the future. This is helpful once again if you are only busy on ice for a brief period—you can draft all of your posts and schedule their publication over the next 2-3 weeks.

Conclusion

Social media campaigns require a lot of effort since so many people really need to see your content, hear of them, often enough to remember and want to follow, and then to create patrons a constant behavior ...

... to social media platforms with the tips prepared in this book, ... and its proper meaning, and ... ... and the ... ...

... remain the different tools, like ... has mentioned, with help you ... choose a sustained and successful social media campaign for your school.

122

14 Monitoring Conversation and Your Reputation

Recall some of our earliest discussions about how often most people in our audience's demographic actually engage through social media. The majority of people on social networks are doing the equivalent of "listening" to conversations about things that interest them. They are not engaging as much as they are watching other people's engagements.

Combine this with the fact that the majority of any type of consumer—potential student or potential car buyer—trusts family and friends most of all, and then the opinions of others posted online over your own trustworthiness.

The upshot is that what others say about you, matters.

As part of your entire strategy you need to find out what is being said about you and by whom. Once you see what is being said in conversations, you can react to it (in the case of misinformation), or provide opportunities for engagement. This strategy is known as Online Reputation Management, or ORM.

1. How to Monitor Conversation

There are a number of tools that help you monitor online conversations. The first of these you have already been introduced to in previous chapters: Google Alerts. This is the simplest tool to use. Simply go to Google Alerts (http://www.google.com/alerts) and create an alert for any number of combinations of your school's name.

You will have to wade through the search results to find anything you really need to reply to, but the time spent doing this is very important.

Look especially for blog posts or news articles that talk about your school, various departments or programs, or even faculty members. When appropriate, comment on the article (using either your Facebook or Twitter username if you can) by either refuting and correcting information, or simply thanking the writer for their attention.

You will find that you are going to be getting a ton of email alerts from a variety of sources. It might be a good idea to create an email presence just to collect these various alerts so your primary inbox does not get filled on a daily basis.

Another tool to use that you have already been introduced to is Twitter Search (http://twitter.search.com). Setting up searches similar to those in Google Alert is easy to do and will deliver conversations happening in Twitter about the subjects you are interested in (in this case, your school, admission process, admission counselors, faculty, etc.).

The element that makes Twitter Search stand apart is the fact that it searches and delivers results in real-time. As soon as someone mentions your school, you are notified and can view the conversation taking place.

Facebook is a bit difficult to monitor because access to users' posts depends on their privacy settings. If their settings are public, however, there are tools to comb through discussions. Facebook's native search tool is found at http://www.facebook.com/search. With it you can search through public posts (which will search both people with public settings and pages), and posts by groups (which have public settings).

Other tools combine all of these functions. Social Mention (http://www.socialmention.com) is one such tool that combines all searches—including Facebook and Twitter searches—in one. You can conduct real-time searches, as well as set up alerts to notify you of new social conversations. It also has features that allow you to analyze the results of any given search you conduct, including the primary keywords used and whether the conversation was positive or negative.

Ultimately, ORM is about research and investigation. The happiest are those who never start down this path because then they will never learn what others are saying about them. But in terms of social media marketing, this is an essential piece of an overall strategy.

You need to know what is being said, good and bad, because it makes such an impact on your audience. Not only for the final decision of what university they might attend, but also which ones they might investigate in the first place.

I am often asked, however, what to do about negative content. How do you handle feedback that is unfair or damaging to your reputation? We discuss that next.

2. Promote the Good and Bury the Bad

The title of this section seems a bit disingenuous. After all, people have a right to see the criticisms for any particular school, right?

The answer, of course, is "yes."

But what do you do about unfair criticism or outright wrong and negative information?

There is always the option of legally going after the person who posted or wrote the information. But that could take years and force you to spend a lot of money in legal costs.

You could also address the information directly, which may prove effective. You could, for example, provide the correct information as a comment. More often than not however the comments are deleted or are in some way used against you. This type of negative engagement is really not the ideal and only serves to promote the person spreading the negative content.

Correctly handling negative content lies in a concept called "curation," which was mentioned in an earlier chapter.

Curation essentially implies that you distribute information to fans, friends and followers that they want to see. Like a curator at a museum, you take it upon yourself to organize and categorize information for others.

While doing this, you are in essence promoting the good, which organically downplays the bad.

The simplest way to curate positive information is simply to spread it to your audience. We have talked about this at length already. Whenever you find positive information about your school—whether it is a blog post or news article—send the link to your fans, friends and followers. You can also promote these articles and blogs in your own blogs.

Remember also that one of the ways Google and other search engines rank information is according to how many links are pointing to pages and sites. The theory then states that if there are more links pointing to the positive information than the bad, the positive will be ranked higher in search engine results (which provide the impetus for linking to those positive articles).

Some professional organizations create social bookmark presences for this express purpose. They collect and tag every available article, video and blog entry that references them, either positive or simply generally informative.

Some even create websites dedicated to the information others have made about them.

Both of these methods increase the online profile of positive information. They also provide methods for your audience or people otherwise interested in you to find information about you. Be careful though, it is always fairly obvious that an organization is merely promoting itself when all of the entries show that organization in a saintly light.

Another method, sometimes used for an especially great piece of information—such as an elevation in school ranking by a trusted ranking body—is creating a viral campaign to promote that information.

When a video or article or image goes viral, there is a good chance that it did not really happen organically as the name would imply. Instead what probably happened was a well-designed campaign of spreading the object in question to blogs, news outlets, etc.

Using mass press-release services like PR Web (http://www.prweb.com), which can distribute a press release with social and multi-media objects—such as videos, images, etc.—organizations can put the item they want to promote in the hands of thousands of content-creators (blog owners or journalists for example).

You can also add the story or video to sites that specialize in viral content, like Buzz Feed (http://www.buzzfeed.com), The Next Web (http://www.thenextweb.com) or News Vine (http://www.newsvine.com). These sites are regularly combed through by journalists and blog owners for interesting or humorous information to add and promote on their own sites.

The combination of these strategies will improve the odds that the stories you want your audience to see will actually be seen.

This is not to say—once again—that we want to mislead people. If there is an article, a blog, a video or other type of content that provides fair and accurate criticism, it would be misleading to try to hide or bury that.

In these cases, use your best judgment. Engaging with honest criticism can be warranted and prove fruitful. If the information is verifiably wrong, you should provide the correct information and a source where the information can be verified. If the information is a true and fair critique of a mistake you made, provide a comment that acknowledges the mistake and assures readers it is not typical and will not happen again. Finally, leave contact information where people can access more details if they choose.

Honesty and integrity online is important, so you want to ensure that you maintain yours. However, helping people find and read accurate and valuable information is helpful not only to you, but to them as well, so make this your goal.

Action Items

1. Create Google Alerts containing your school's name.

2. Create a saved Twitter search with your school's name.

3. Do the results contain any negative information? Is that information fair or unfair?

4. Do a search in Google with the name of your school, plus the terms "sucks" and see if anything appears. How should you handle the information you find?

15 Measuring your Return on Investment

It is hard to know where to place this in the order of materials for this book, but understanding your Return on Investment (ROI) is vitally important because it helps give you a compass for establishing goals and objectives.

The ROI of any campaign is typically based on the number of *conversions* the campaign results in.

A conversion is any action the target of a campaign takes that converts that person from a prospect to a customer/user/member. The conversion someone is interested in could be the purchase of an item, or it could be simply clicking a link.

We measure the amount of money spent on a campaign (our investment) against how many of these conversions we get as a result of our efforts (our return).

Understanding the ROI for social media campaigns is not at all easy, however.

The main problem is in how and when conversion takes place. Unlike a simple mass email campaign, which could lead to direct sales or links clicked, social media campaigns are ongoing and typically very slow.

We do not advertise and therefore do not carry out short burst-like campaigns, but instead we make friends and create relationships to draw in our students.

Thus, conversions do not happen right away, and they are often not directly attributable to our efforts through social media. We will typically see little feedback or progress until all of a sudden we see really large and very unusual gains all at once.

I will give you an example of what I mean. When I began an aggressive social media marketing campaign in August of 2009, New Mexico Tech had just had two straight years of declining enrollments.

In 2010 we saw record enrollments that had administrators scrambling to find dorms to house all of the new students and to create new classes for them to take as sections quickly filled. We saw a similar increase in 2011.

We campaigned through social media for almost a year before seeing any results, and then some could argue that they were not directly attributable to our social media strategies (though no other strategies had changed).

This is something you should expect. Unfortunately, many others expect social media marketing to resemble the tired marketing strategies of the past. They will want demonstrable results and conversion as their ROI.

This simply is not going to happen and it will be up to you to explain why.

But while there is not any ROI which is explicitly conversion-based, there are other measurements that you can use to create your ROI standards. Here are three examples that you can use.

- Number of Followers, Friends or Connections
- Direct Engagement
- Indirect Engagement

1. Number of Followers, Friends or Connections

This is a measurement that I do not really subscribe to, but many do and it is easy for those who do not understand social media marketing to grasp.

I do not particularly care for it because it is so artificial. After all, it is easy to spend a couple of thousand dollars to buy a few thousand followers on Twitter, but what does it matter if they are not going to ever go to your school or refer others to you?

This is a point mentioned in an earlier chapter regarding our goals for social media marketing.

The ROI should measure not only the number of people that follow you on Twitter, Facebook or other networks, but their quality as well. Are they your primary demographic (students)? Do they influence your primary demographic (such as parents, friends, etc.)? If so, these are quality followers.

Measure the number of followers in comparison to who you want to be followed by. Then you can create an ROI benchmark every month that tracks your new followers, friends and connections, as well as their quality.

In fact, you could come up with a chart that specifically places your primary demographic of followers (potential students) in one category, your secondary demographic (influencers) in another category, and all others in a third category. It might look something like the following:

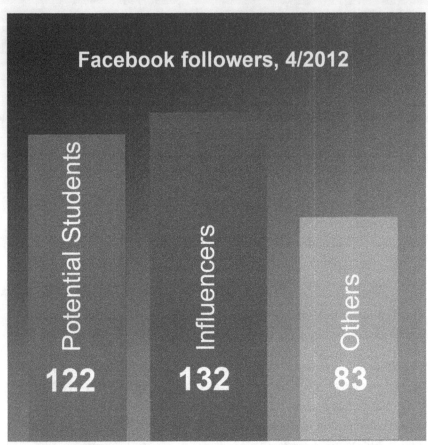

A benchmark chart demonstrating a monthly report of followers and their quality.

It is important to make clear to stakeholders who want to see these statistics how you are measuring followers and why, otherwise the whole strategy and campaign effort is completely lost.

2. Direct Engagement

Another good measurement to use, and one that I use frequently, is the amount of direct engagements you receive over the course of a month. This takes into consideration the following:

- Number of replies to tweets
- Number of comments to status posts
- Number of comments to videos, pictures or links shared

It does not stop there, however. During the course of these replies and comments you should counter with your own thoughts or feedback.

This in fact, is crucial, because this is what takes social media from the one-sided broadcast mechanism and places it in the conversation medium—the whole point of social media in the first place.

Remember that each time you fully engage with one of your potential students, or one of their influencers, you are moving the potential student closer to you—taking them from the "potential student" to the "new student" category. At the same time you are also creating an interaction that others are watching, that majority of social media users who simply hang back and listen to the conversations going on around them.

So your ROI could take into consideration direct engagement—comments, replies, etc.—and then also have a separate measurement or standard for conversations. In fact, the combination of these statistics could be the primary measurement you to use for your ROI.

3. Indirect Engagement

This measurement looks specifically at the number of times, and the various methods, that your content is engaged by friends and followers, but which has engagement not of the direct kind.

In other words, this records the number of Likes or Shares (Facebook), Retweets and Mentions (Twitter) and other indirect engagement forms that your content brings.

The general rule is that 20% of the users of any given network will create 80% of the content—including comments and postings. So, at any given time 80% of the users—your friends, fans and followers—are completely silent.

However, there is a tendency to "like" something over commenting, because it is easier and not as concrete as putting your name next to text. Similarly, sharing content—by retweeting or sharing it with your friends—is much easier than engaging you or that content.

Therefore, experts suggest that more often than not, those "lurkers" who do not create tweets or posts themselves, and who are not willing to engage with you in conversation, are more likely to "Like" something.

This measurement then, is a really good indicator of the general popularity of your content, and really helps to let you know if you are sharing the correct information.

In conclusion, these three ROI measurements should be outlined in your strategy (which we look at next) and tracked over the course of the year to give you a good idea of your progress. As the number of friends, followers and fans grows, you will begin to see results in the form of more enrollments, more campus tour requests, more information requests, etc.

As you see upticks in these real conversion measurements (enrollment number, etc.), look at the long-term progress of your social media campaign.

Ideally, as students enroll, you can somehow track them through a questionnaire to find out if they are already friends, fans or followers, and when they became so.

The combination of this information will give you a definitive measurement of your campaign, and let you adjust your strategy accordingly.

Action Items

1. Create a ROI strategy and define what you will use to define the ROI of your campaign.

2. Identify the members of your school that you will have to report the results of your campaign to.

3. Next to each of the names from number 2, note the proficiency or knowledge each has about social media—its use, purpose and general strategy.

4. Finally, look at the ROI strategy again and determine if what you write in number 3 changes what you will report and how.

16 Creating a Strategic Effort

To this point we have looked at social media strategy and platforms in a sort of vacuum. In other words, we have looked at each network—Facebook, Twitter, YouTube, etc.—by itself and without any relation to other platforms. We have looked at the idea of sharing information among different platforms, but we have not really looked at them in relation to each other.

We also have not really talked about what to do with these platforms. Sure we have talked about using them and the best practice and strategies for each, but we have not really looked at using them to fulfill any specific objectives.

This chapter connects the various platforms together into comprehensible strategies you can use to create a sustainable and long-term campaign. You must absolutely create a strategy before you start using social media for your school. Without a strategy, you will not know what you are trying to accomplish, how to accomplish it, or whether or not you ever succeeded.

That is what we will try to do in this chapter then: figure out what you want to do, figure out how to do it, and then figure out whether or not you succeeded. Each of these is a piece of your social media strategy.

We will start first by not even talking about social media. Instead we will talk about what you want to accomplish: your goals and objectives.

Step 1: What do you want to do? Goals and Objectives

The starting point for creating any type of social media strategy—which is crucial for using social media in your school in the first place—is asking what you want to do with it. Why do you want to use it in the first place? What do you hope to accomplish?

Many, many organizations, from businesses to government agencies, have rushed into social media only to find that it just "does not work for them." And then they subsequently lose interest and stop using it altogether. Ultimately they are surpassed by their competition and must spend much more money to catch up and use social media correctly.

The problem though is that they never sit down and ask, "Well what is the definition of 'working' in the first place?" They never really understand what they want to do with it.

The problem, I think, stems from the belief that social media is like other, older forms of marketing—that it is like advertising. We covered this at the beginning of this book, though, and know that social media is vastly different than traditional forms of marketing.

So let us start by asking what you want to accomplish with your social media use. Do you want to simply increase enrollment? Do you want to ensure that applicants are of a certain quality (maybe test standards), or have a certain interest (science versus athletics)?

These goals are substantially different after all. If you want each of these, you should create different independent strategies for each.

Also keep in mind that—of all the things social media is good for—it is not the best platform for straight conversions.

In other words, people do not simply "buy" things through social media. Instead, they buy from the organization after building the necessary relationship.

It took my school almost a year to really see results from our campaigns and strategies, but we did see results—tremendous results.

So if your goal is something simple, like "increase enrollment" then you need to ensure you have given yourself the proper amount of time to see this goal through.

Next, make sure your goals and objectives are measurable. A goal like, "we want to increase enrollment" is simple enough, but does not have enough information to be measurable. By what percentage do you want to increase enrollment?

Instead, make your goal, "we want to increase enrollment by 15% over the previous three years' averages."

This gives you not only a target to hit—15%—but also a measurement by which to compare (the previous three years' measurement).

Now modify the goal even further by adding a deadline. Make the deadline realistic—remember that it takes time to enact the strategies we have covered here. With all of these things in place your goal would read like the following:

We want to increase enrollment by 15% over the previous three years' averages by August 2014.

Do not be afraid to have multiple goals, in fact you should. Just remember that each will demand its own strategy and campaign.

Step 2: Who is Your Audience and what do you know about them?

The next step is to understand who you are trying to engage with. Again, you can have multiple audiences to devote your campaigns to, but you need a different strategy for each. Here are some potential audiences you will probably want to create engagement with:

- Potential students
- Parents of potential students
- High school counselors
- Friends of potential students

Next, narrow these audiences down as far as you possibly can. For example, you can focus on potential students in a certain area, going to a specific high school, or playing on a specific high school sports team.

The same goes for any other audience you can think of. The more focused and narrow you can make this, the more successful your strategy will be.

Next, list as much as you possibly can about each audience. You may want to ask questions about them to help you understand more. Some questions could include:

- Where do they live?
- What hobbies or interests do they have?
- What motivates them?
- What do they want out of a school or university?
- What is their economic situation?
- What future goals or objectives do they have?
- What kind of career are they hoping for?

The answers to these questions—and any others you can think of—will help you narrow your focus even further and target your approach. These answers will help determine the types of posts you create, videos you make and blogs you write.

For example, if you understand that cost is a big factor in determining what school they are interested in, you can post more often about how to get financial aid, where to find scholarship information, FAFSA mistakes that people make, etc. And, as we have discussed, you can pepper these types of posts with the occasional mention of the value of your school or the grant and financial aid opportunities found there.

You also need to determine what social media platforms your audience (or audiences) is (are) most often using. Are they on Facebook or Twitter more often? Are they reading blogs or watching videos on YouTube more often?

The answer to these questions will help you identify where to focus your attention if not on all platforms. After all, you really do not want to waste time or effort on social media networks that your audience is not even using or paying attention to.

We know some of the answers from our previous chapters. We know, for example, that our main demographic—potential students between 14 and 17—makes up the third largest group of users on Facebook. We also know that they account for much of the traffic and video views on YouTube.

But you need to know more than these generalities. You need to know, for example, if the specific group of students you have targeted actually fits into these statistics. What if the students you are targeting belong to the small group of people in that demographic who frequently use Twitter?

You also need to know about audiences other than just the potential students. Where do their parents or high school counselors spend the most time? Is it on Facebook or YouTube as well?

Understanding your audience well enough to engage them will take research on your part, so devote time to this step. Without the answers to the questions we have asked here you could end up wasting even more time in the long run.

Step 3: Match your Platforms to your Goals and Audience

Now that you understand what the goals and objectives are for your social media marketing campaign, and you have taken the time to understand all there is to know about your audience, you can begin thinking about what platforms you want to use to achieve your results.

You might be asking yourself, "But we just went over all the platforms to use, did not we?"

Yes, we did. We went over the available platforms to use, and we looked more narrowly at the top four that will help your campaign, but that does not mean that you can or should use them all. There are a couple of reasons for this.

First of all, you never want to make a half-hearted attempt at social media marketing. This is an all-or-nothing method of reaching people, after all. If you cannot devote enough time and effort to each platform equally, and that time and effort is not enough to use any given one as it should be used, then you really should not even try a social media marketing campaign in the first place.

Does this sound too harsh? It may, but it is the unfortunate reality.

Remember that social media is not advertising, it is a conversation. If you do not participate in a conversation then what happens? People forget you are there, or they begin talking to someone else.

Likewise, what happens when you begin a conversation with someone and then just stop talking to them? That person will most likely think you rude, strange or both.

In either case what are the chances that the person will actually want to start up another conversation with you?

The best idea is to limit yourself to what you can spend the most time on and just focus on those one or two platforms. Twitter, for example, is very time-consuming, and if you decide to create a Twitter presence you should be willing to spend a couple of hours every day devoted to tweeting and searching Twitter.

Next, only establish a presence on those platforms that your audience is actually using. This sounds pretty obvious, right? Well then why do so many places decide to go all in: Facebook, Twitter, YouTube, LinkedIn, etc, etc, then neglect almost all of them, losing them credibility and their potential audience?

Probably because they were told by some "expert" that they should set them all up to be competitive.

Unfortunately this just is not true.

While having a presence on all of the platforms has some advantages, it makes little sense to spend time and energy on every platform if nobody is actually even looking at them.

Focusing only on platforms that your audience is using will also help you understand and grasp many of the concepts about social media that confuse people. You will find in short time that you have mastered Facebook or another, and can quickly apply that knowledge to a different platform.

This will, of course, also require you to really look at that question in the previous step: what are the main platforms your audience is using?

You can find out through interviews and surveys with entering freshmen, ask them at traditional recruiting events, and simply use search engine research. Knowing is crucial to the success of your strategy.

Step 4: Create Posting Guidelines and Schedules

You should devote time to writing down the planned frequency of posts, articles or videos that you will be making.

If you are creating Facebook posts or Twitter updates, you should list how often those will be made. Facebook posts are usually targeted, and the frequency can range from one to three times a day.

Twitter updates are much more frequent and users typically create anywhere from five or six to well over a dozen every day.

You can also plan what media—images, videos, etc.—you can or will share. Write down the specific sites you will get content from, what Google Alerts you have set up, and what Twitter searches you have saved.

Try to get updates—especially on Google Alerts—at the very start of the day so you can spread out what you post.

Also create a consistent time-schedule for both blog articles and YouTube videos.

Blog articles should be written and posted at least once a week, but the more the better. Remember that Google will index content when it finds it. If it finds it, and it is new, it will come back more frequently to see if there is any more new content. The more often it finds new content, the more often your site will be indexed. This means that your site will more often be included in search query results and you will be more likely to be read.

The case is similar with videos. The more often you create and post videos, the more often your content will show up in search engine query results, or in YouTube search results (remember that YouTube is the second most often used search engine).

I would advise that when starting out you post at least two blog articles every week for the first year, and at least one video per week for that long as well. Within about 7-8 months you will see a dramatic rise in the number of visits your site and your articles start receiving.

At the very least, you must try as hard as you can to be as consistent as possible. Post often, but post like clockwork—especially the blog articles and YouTube videos. Believe it or not, audience members will start looking for you to post new tidbits, and will wander away if you veer off from your schedule.

Also, remember not to just stop at any point, keep posting/updating/filming/writing. If, however, you do have to go on hiatus for any reason, let your followers and fans know so they will not simply lose interest and leave.

Step 5: Determine Roles and Time

Who exactly is going to be doing the posting to Facebook? To Twitter?

Who will be writing the blog articles and creating the videos?

Enacting a full strategy is a lot of work for one person, and so I would not suggest going down that route. Instead, make it an office or department initiative, with everyone given an assigned role or multiple roles. This not only makes it easier (overall), but it also makes the campaign more fun and ultimately more successful.

Likewise, make sure that the people who are carrying out your initiative have multiple roles instead of compartmentalizing them into single roles. Ensure that everyone is taught exactly how to use each platform in the context of marketing, and also make sure everyone understands your objectives.

Many schools and universities use students in roles concerning social media. This is certainly allowable, and maybe even preferred (considering their identification with one of the school's target audiences). But if this is the case make sure they have the proper training, and that they understand both your goals and objectives and how to un-market on the various platforms you use.

Even when assigning multiple roles you must still designate a single person for each platform to schedule content and make sure that your schedule is followed. You certainly do not want to repeat effort when it is not needed and you need a clear sense of who is the administrator for each platform you use.

Remember that this is a daily effort. For each platform someone must not only be creating your content—which is the portion of effort most everyone pays attention to—but they must also be measuring your effectiveness.

Step 6: Measurement and Revision

The portion of social media marketing that really gets all of the attention is the interaction and the engagement—the posting and updating. Organizations keep a careful eye on when the last post was made, the last article was written, or the last video was created and uploaded.

Most organizations also look at measurement in terms of how many fans, followers or subscribers they have. How quickly are they gaining new followers in comparison to competitors?

What many do not realize is that there is another layer of measurement that needs to be considered: engagement and interaction.

We covered this in the chapter discussing ROI. As we stated there, understanding what you are getting out of your effort must be more than the simplest of variables—how many fans or followers you have.

Because we are discussing a very complex and complicated strategy—marketing via personal relationships—we must necessarily understand that the variables for measuring this will likewise be complex and complicated.

However, measurement is crucial to an ongoing effort because without it you are simply throwing money away.

So create a measurement section in your strategy by asking this question: what variables will determine if our goal is being achieved?

If it is simply to increase enrollment of a certain population of students by a certain date, then begin there.

In that case you would not only look at the number of fans or followers, you would also look at their quality to determine if you are attracting those you want to attract.

For example, that are their ages? Where do they live? What are their likes or interests? What other brands or organizations are they following? What do they post about or tweet about?

Not all of this information will be readily available—much of it will depend on their privacy settings. But typically about 2/3 of your fans and followers will have enough information made public to get a sense of your progress.

Next, measure your engagements and interactions. How often are you talking to your fans and followers? What is the quality of these interactions? What is it gaining you?

Using your findings from these measurements, you should then begin looking at how you can improve your strategy. Where and how should you shift your focus and effort? Should you put more time into Twitter? Are blogs as effective as you thought?

This portion of the strategy is the most difficult because it actually requires the most time. It is ongoing and complicated, and it requires effort that quite frankly is not that visible. When we do not see people working, or the results of that work, it is sometimes tough to really believe they are working at all.

Conclusion

You have made it! You have gained a formal understanding of social media marketing, the differences between social media marketing and advertising, and you know how to un-market. You have also looked at how to use the most effective platforms and which ones hold your audience. You understand now how your audiences use these platforms and how you can reach them.

You have also created a strategy for your organization to use, narrowing your audience and clearly defining your goals and objectives. You have created a schedule and assigned roles, and now you are ready to begin.

So, begin! Take the next step and start engaging people. You have learned to use the newest and most important technology for the future of higher education recruiting and admission, all you need to do now it put it to work!

References

1. http://admissionblog.usc.edu/2011/09/27/day-in-the-life/

2. https://www.noellevitz.com/NR/rdonlyres/52057241-5FD7-450E-8399-C772C1F9A3F9/0/EExpectations_FocusingYourERecruitmentEfforts_0710.pdf

3. http://mashable.com/2009/12/23/pepsi-super-bowl/

4. http://www.socialmediaexaminer.com/SocialMediaMarketingReport2011.pdf?9d7bd4

5. http://www.forbes.com/sites/roberthof/2011/08/26/online-ad-spend-to-overtake-tv/

6. http://www.focus.com/images/view/58313/

7. http://www.altimetergroup.com/

8. http://syncapse.com/white-paper-understanding-facebook-fan-value-a-study-of-key-roi-indicators-and-values-for-leading-brand-marketers/

9. http://www.constantcontact.com/small-business-week/survey-fall-2011.jsp

10. http://www.constantcontact.com/small-business-week/survey.jsp

11. http://blog.nielsen.com/nielsenwire/online_mobile/friends-following-and-feedback-how-were-using-social-media/

12. http://www.pewinternet.org/Reports/2010/Social-Media-and-Young-Adults.aspx

13. http://socialmediatoday.com/kenburbary/276356/facebook-demographics-revisited-2011-statistics

14. http://www.pewinternet.org/Commentary/2010/November/Pew-Internet-Data-Provides-Context-for-the-Facebook-Messages-Announcement.aspx

15. http://www-935.ibm.com/services/uk/cio/pdf/social_media_Part_Executive_Report.pdf

16. http://blog.nielsen.com/nielsenwire/consumer/global-advertising-consumers-trust-real-friends-and-virtual-strangers-the-most/

17. http://blog.nielsen.com/nielsenwire/online_mobile/three-screen-report-q409/

18. http://www.optify.net/seo/why-do-seo/

Index

www.ingramcontent.com/pod-product-compliance
Lightning Source LLC
Chambersburg PA
CBHW071158050326
40689CB00011B/2159